THE GRINGO GUIDE TO PANAMA II

More to Know Before You Go

JuliAnne Murphy

THE GRINGO GUIDE TO PANAMA II

More to Know Before You Go

DEDICATION

For my fellow adventurer, Tom, who packed his bags without a backward glance and accompanied me on this crazy chapter of what became life in Panama. He was the *"Tú"* to my *"Yo"* for many, many years and I will forever cherish the time we enjoyed together.

PREFACE

WHEN THIS BOOK was first published in early 2014, only a year had passed since I had written the first in the Gringo Guide to Panama series, *The Gringo Guide to Panama: What to Know Before You Go.*

I had no idea when I published that first guide if anyone would have the slightest interest in its contents. Happily, it's been a huge success: the book became a bestseller on Amazon less than a month after publication. It's popularity among those looking to move to Panama or retire in Panama proved that there was indeed a market for sharing this type of practical, personal information from the viewpoint of an expat who's already been there, done that. And, that first book about Panama, also paved the way for many, many other bloggers and writers about Panama who have come on the scene since.

When you live in a place like Panama (or perhaps anywhere that is not your native-born home), your day-to-day experiences become the stories shared around your dinner table. Your stories are unique; they become part of who you are. They also become a mechanism for learning how to cope and thrive.

After my first book hit bestseller, the follow-up questions from my readers began to pour in to my website at www. PanamaGringoGuide.com. *How hard is it to find a home in Panama? What schools should I be considering? What's the best way to bring my pets with me? What things do I need to know about doing business in Panama? What does Panama offer to retirees? What is the healthcare system like? Is it easy to travel to and from Panama?*

Between 2012 and 2015, I blogged about my day-to-day experiences in Panama, in addition to interacting on Google+ and Twitter with the outside world. In addition to my own anecdotes, I interviewed a number of local expats about their experiences. I've also been fortunate to be interviewed, write guest posts, and answer numerous questions for others interested in Panama.

Some say there are three distinct phases one goes through in acclimating to life as an expat in the Republic of Panama. Phase One encompasses the first two years when you learn how to survive and find your way around. Phase Two is when you're figuring out if you really like the country. And Phrase Three is when you've become a seasoned expat.

This third phase is the vantage point from where I wrote this book, the second in the Gringo Guide to Panama series, after six years of living in Panama. A quirky mix of Westerner and tropicalized mentality is what you'll notice in the unique perspectives I express in this book. (Note that Phases One and Two are covered in my first book in the series.)

I was fortunate to call the Republic of Panama home for eight years, from 2008 to early 2016. After several years of living here, we did a lot more laughing than grinding our teeth when things didn't go our way in day-to-day life. We became much more proficient at a variety of water sports. And, mostly, we just adapted pretty darn well to life in Panama as expats. We felt fortunate as such.

As with the first book in the Gringo Guide to Panama series, I hope that this second book will be exactly what it's titled for you and yours – *More* to Know Before You Go as you explore and research and find out if this quirky little country is a good fit for *you*.

Note that this book does *not* replace the first in the Gringo Guide to Panama series. In fact, I recommend you get that and read it first, as I refer to it frequently here. The first book essentially serves as a base for this one.

In the pages that follow, you'll get a recap of what has been said about Panama in recent years (that most Gringos don't know), plus an insider's perspective on where to stay when you come visit, why Panama is so attractive for the retiring set, and a realistic view of Panama's healthcare system. Learn what questions to ask of your mover, of your real estate broker, and how to plug into local life, once you arrive. Don't miss the realities I outline for living in a tropical climate either – this is one of those things people really don't consider before they move, but it is so important. Also included is some key information on doing business in Panama, traveling, and interviews from other expats.

I wish you all the best on *your* Panama journey, or wherever you may land.

CONTENTS

1

Panama Today:
What's it really like?

Street scene in Santa Ana, 2013.

FOR YEARS, WHEN people learned we lived in Panama, their first response would be, *"Wow! What took you down there? Is that crazy dictator Noriega still in power?"* The second comment would be, *"Oh, right! I've always wanted to come see the Panama Canal. What's that like?"* And lastly, *"Is Panama safe?"*

All of these queries are clear indications to me that most North Americans still don't have a clue about Panama in today's world.

In the past ten years, this little *país* (country) has grown and expanded and morphed substantially. In my opinion, Panama really came into its own in the past five years. And, while many people will today say, *"Oh, yeah, I read something about Panama. Things are really happening down there."* If you press them, they really don't know much more than that. If you're new to all things Panama, here are a few things you may not have realized about the country with the smallest population in Latin America (according to Wikipedia, January 2015).

- Panama uses the U.S. dollar, which means there's no exchange rate to worry about if you are from the U.S.

- In 2013, Panama was rated the safest country in Central America by the U.S. State Department, because of its low level of violent crime. As of March 2015, the State Department website lists Panama's crime rating as High, with the accompanying sentence, "Panama remains relatively safe when compared to other Central American countries, although crime rates are higher than one would encounter in much of the U.S." (Refer to this diplomatic report at http://www.osac.gov and search for Panama 2015 Crime and Safety Report for specifics.)

- Panama has the best road infrastructure in Central America, making travel within its borders easier than in most developing nations in the region.

- Foreigners have the same legal rights as locals when it comes to owning real estate.

- Panama offers permanent residency visas to North Americans with investments as low as $5,000, with the recent passage of the new Friendly Nations visa in 2012.

Why are so many people choosing Panama?
Many find Panama more affordable than living in the U.S.
Prior to 2008, the largest number of expats moving to Panama came from the U.S. With the global downturn since that time, most U.S. citizens have lower liquidity for making investments outside, and that number has declined. In late 2012, with President Obama's re-election, more U.S. citizens are again actively seeking other options. And for many, Panama is at the top of the list.

Are you dreaming of a tropical life?
What is it about Panama that makes it so appealing to Westerners looking to move or retire? In 2013 and 2014, Panama was rated the happiest country in the world according to a survey conducted by Gallup. In 2015, Panama ranked #25 in the world according to a similar study by the United Nations. (Here's an interesting comparison of those two studies, from the U.N.'s website: http://www.gallup. com/opinion/gallup/182843/happiest-people-world-swiss-lat-in-americans.aspx).

Many Westerners love the idea of a more relaxed pace. Would you enjoy living where the beach is just an hour's drive away from your city? Or living in a country where the frenetic pace of "keeping up with the Joneses" is not a priority? Does a tropical climate with summer-like weather on a year-round basis appeal to you?

Are you interested in a more affordable cost of living?
What makes retiring in Panama so amenable to many Westerners? The country's Jubilado program for retirees is very compelling for those living on a fixed budget. The cost of many available services in Panama is generally much lower than similar costs in many other countries.

Panama is easily accessible from the U.S.
Panama is easy to travel to. Its international airport is undergoing a major expansion, and has direct flights to many cities in the U.S. and Canada, as well as to every capital city in Latin America and the Caribbean.

Panama has decent roadway and transportation systems.
Panama's roadway system is the best in Central America. In the city, Panama opened the first leg of its new metro system in 2014 – the first of its kind in Central America. A second leg is under construction in 2015, and three other lines are planned.

Indeed, road infrastructure in the city in the past five years in Panama has expanded tremendously. In January 2016, the country announced a pact with Japan to construct a high-speed monorail system from the city's Western suburbs into downtown.

Panama is a safe place to live.
Panama is a very safe country. Serious crime like rapes and murder are not commonplace. Theft and pickpocketing do

happen, especially in tourist areas, but overall, expats say they feel more comfortable in Panama than in other Latin American countries relevant to safety concerns.

Want to learn more?
Because Panama appears sophisticated in so many ways, many Westerners seeking to move or retire here often neglect to conduct appropriate due diligence on the country. But your research is important to ensure that your experience of living in Panama is realistic. *The Gringo Guide to Panama: What to Know Before You Go* should be your first reference. The book you have in your hand is the second in the Gringo Guide to Panama series, and while it holds very valuable information, will best be understood with the first book in the series already under your belt.

Slums in Santa Ana

Panama's Recent Rankings:
What do they mean to you?

Everywhere you look in recent years, Panama is like a rising star. People are talking about it. Some say Panama is the new hot place for North Americans seeking to escape the U.S (for whatever reason). The economy has not only remained stable in Panama over the past ten years, it has grown! The World Bank reports positive economic growth between 4% and 12% over the past nine years, with 2014 at 6.2%. Similar rates are projected in 2016 and 2017.

You're obviously curious because you're reading this book, right? But all the stories – all the news articles – all the glowing reports about Panama…what do they *really* mean to someone who's considering moving here?

Well, they may be relevant, and they may not. It really depends on *why* you're considering Panama for yourself. But, for your reference, here's a list of some of the most recent rankings and stories about Panama, so you can see them for yourself.

The Miraflores Locks on the Panama Canal

Reports and stories about Panama have appeared in some of the world's leading news sources in the past five years, including the following:

- *Panama City Rising* (New York Times, May 2, 2013): An overview by Tim Neville of Panama City's growth and expansion in the past 13 years which likens Panama to "a major leisure destination in record time."

- *What are the most expensive cities to live in?* (CNN.com, Feb. 4, 2013): Panama ranked #8 in the Ten *Least* expensive cities to live in, in the world, according to the latest Worldwide Cost of Living Survey from the Economist Intelligence Unit. (www.eiu.com)

- *Panama City, Mission Viejo* (New York Times, Sept. 16, 2012): Fred A. Bernstein evaluates the rapid changes in Panama's old city (Casco Viejo), which are threatening the area's UNESCO heritage status. "A pro-construction ethos seems to be in Panama's DNA – fitting, perhaps, for a country founded on a civil-engineering project."

- *Parents in Tow, Finding a Charming and Cheap Corner of Panama* (New York Times, January 21, 2016): Seth Kugel reports on recent travel seeking the less traveled road. http://www.nytimes.com/2016/01/21/travel/parents-in-tow-finding-a-charming-and-cheap-corner-of-panama.html

- *Doing Business 2016 rankings* The World Bank and the International Finance Corporation): Panama ranked 69 out of 189 countries, though #1 out of all countries in Central America for ease of doing business (i.e. starting a firm).

- *Panama Cost of Living* (http://www.Xpatulator.com): The current overall cost of living rank for the country of Panama is 129 out of 217 countries as of October 2016. (The U.S. is listed at 110 as a point of reference and Ecuador is listed at 156.) (For transferring expats, this website rates Panama City with a "Some Hardship" ranking, which they equate to a 20% premium. See the website for further explanation.)
- *The World's 21 Best Cities for Retirement* (U.S. News & World Report, June 2013): Kathleen Peddicourt of Live & Invest Overseas rates the Panama City beach area in the Republic of Panama as one of *"the best places to retire to the beach in the company of fellow expat retirees."*
- *Panama: Best Countries for Business* (Forbes.com, December 2015): Panama ranked #56 out of 180 countries worldwide.
- *2016 Global Retirement Index* (International Living): Panama continues to rank #1. (I have to be honest here – I hesitate to include anything in my book by IL. While I know and adore their country correspondent in Panama, I find that the group's representation of this country is mostly lollipops and sunshine, which is not at all realistic in my experience of living in Panama as a whole. In fact, many expats tell me they find it misleading. That said, IL's publications and reports are widely read, so please take what you read of theirs with a grain of salt.)

- The CIA reports a World Fact Book on every country in the world. If you're interested in statistics, this has all kinds of them: https://www.cia.gov/library/publications/the-world-factbook/geos/pm.html

So, what's it all *mean*? Ultimately, it means Panama has become a place worthy of consideration, depending on what criteria you have on your checklist. But, for you as a new (or future) expat, this only *begins* your homework. It's up to you to dig in, to find out if Panama is really for *you*, and if it measures up to what you're really looking for. Only *you* can ultimately answer that question. This book (and its predecessor book in the Gringo Guide to Panama series) will help you find the answers to the questions you don't even know you have yet about life in Panama. And, getting a realistic picture of all those things will help you figure out if a move to Panama is really right for you, or not.

Read on.

2

PANAMA 101: HOW DOES IT COMPARE TO THE DEVELOPED WORLD?

Many reports on living in Panama only give a pie in the sky perspective

IN THIS CHAPTER, you'll read about some of the basics about Panama, which you may or may not already know. But first, so that you get a better feel of what Panama is like, I'll start off with my story.

My Story

I lived in Panama for eight years, from early 2008 to early 2016. My family and I relocated here from the U.S. when I was recruited to come to Panama for a new position working for an international firm. I lived adjacent to the city of Panama, which is the only large metropolis in the country (1.6 million as of 2016), and my former husband and I both worked in the same area, during our time living in-country. (The city of Panama is like New York City – locals only refer to it as Panama, Panama and don't actually use the word 'city.')

When you come to Panama as a foreigner, you generally have four options. First, you can come in and out on a tourist visa, which is good for up to six months. Second, you can get a temporary work visa, which is renewable every one to three years (and to which your residency in the country is tied). Third, you can apply for a permanent work or residency visa (one such example would be the Friendly Nations visa). Fourth, you can renounce your citizenship from whence you came (which means giving up your passport and all your rights of being a citizen of that country) and apply for a Panamanian passport.

We fell into the third option. We are U.S. citizens, maintain our U.S. passports and citizenship, and also have our Panamanian cédulas (or permanent residency cards).

When we originally came to Panama, we thought of the opportunity to live and work in Panama as an adventure. We thought we'd stay for two to three years. Boy, were we wrong! We stayed beyond that partly due to the professional success we found in Panama and because we learned to enjoy life in this tiny country.

Professional Opportunity

The professional opportunities we found here are almost unlimited. Because this is a developing nation, many of the industries and services you get accustomed to in the U.S. do not exist yet. Or they are coming, but there's little competition. That's the reason Panama has begun to emerge in the minds of so many multinational companies in the past few years – because of that opportunity. And, of course, it's the gateway for global commerce (via the Panama Canal) and a way to reach all of the growing Latin American market via the country's central location. The Canal is currently undergoing a $5.2 million expansion, which when complete (est. mid 2016) will triple its current capacity. This means even more possibilities exist for commerce and business in the next few years, and beyond.

The Views

The photos you'll see of Panama (the city) show the impressive skyline, and the Canal. Promotional websites laud the international banking system, affordable real estate and flashy hotels. A few years ago, the actor known as the Rock (Dwayne Johnson) was in Panama filming the Heroes TV series (an extreme sports show). When that season went live, one of the shows included the Rock rappelling off of the Trump Tower here in the city, with some pretty fantastic views.

Two seasons of the popular U.S. TV series *Survivor* have been filmed in Panama in past years: one in Bocas del Toro, on the Caribbean side, and the other in the Pearl Islands on the Pacific side. The world also got a glimpse of Panama when the country hosted the Miss Universe pageant, showcasing the lovely contestants in bikinis on virgin beachfronts.

All of this exposure over the years has provided only the glossy magazine front cover of the country. That's all well and good, but what's it like to really *live* here as an expat? Of course, the answer to that can't be summed up in one paragraph (just like your life elsewhere can't), but here's a few more stats, which most expats want to know when they're considering Panama for their new home.

Language

The official language in Panama is Spanish. About 15% of the native population speak English in some way, shape or form. Which means that the rest of the population does *not*. In the city of Panama and in the touristy areas – the hotels and the touristy restaurants – you'll find you can get along without any Spanish. But in the rest of your life (if you move to Panama), you'll find you need it. It's that simple. (I talk more about this in my first book.)

Education

Panama's public school system is one of the most poorly rated systems in the world, and thus is not an option for most expats with school-aged children. A number of international-level private schools are available, however, with a variety of curriculums and costs. For more on school options, see Chapter 7.

Standard of Living
Real Estate

If you move here from the U.S. or from Europe, or a more developed country, you'll likely be pretty taken aback at the available real estate. Yes, the photos you will find on websites are lovely and taken from the best angles and so forth. They are *promotional*, after all. However, the quality of construction in this country is very different from any of those places. The methods of building here can assure that the structural capability may be safe to live in; however, Panama struggles when it comes to sophisticated finishes – both interiors and exteriors. When you find really nice finishes, or nicer construction, you can expect that it will come at a premium, because it's a limited commodity.

This means three things for expats when they rent or buy a place in Panama:

- You can definitely find affordable real estate, but it's important to personally visit before you purchase. Take time to get every bit of information you can about the developer, the construction of the home or condominium, the neighborhood, the home itself, and the warranty on the property (if new).
- Look at what the offer is to make sure that what you are getting is worth the price you'll be asked to pay. And, be triple sure to have a title search run to confirm that the person offering the property has legal title, and can legally transfer it to you. (There's been too many

scams in years past with Gringos who have not done their homework. The responsibility is yours.)

- You can expect that when something is *really* nice – the price will also be much higher than anything else you see. This is because really nice properties are limited, and therefore, come at a premium.

Now, at the same time, where else can you live – in an urban city, in the Tropics – and have a high-rise, spectacular view of the Pacific Ocean? Right. So, there's a trade-off.

You'll read more on real estate including details on choosing a home and a real estate broker in Chapter 11.

Food and Services

Your food bill will run about the same as what you'd pay for the same foods in many cities in the U.S. That's because processed foods or anything packaged has to be shipped in. Very few foodstuffs are manufactured in Panama. But, your fresh fruits, vegetables and all kinds of fish and chicken are all grown locally and those will be cheap. We found it balanced out in our household, and our grocery bill was about the same as it was each week back home in Denver. Other expats report their bills are higher. It all depends from whence you've come.

The meat counter at a local supermarket

For services, you're in luck. Labor is far cheaper in Panama than it is in the U.S. Which means you can afford luxuries you couldn't back home – a full-time maid, a driver, a gardener, weekly massages, $20 haircuts, and so on. This alone makes Panama really attractive for a lot of people, and it's one of the lifestyle advantages the culture offers.

I cover more on these topics in Chapter 12.

Safety & Security

Is Panama safe? Yes, it is. It is an adjustment for most expats to see uniformed officers on the street with rifles, bulletproof vests and machine guns, but this is the norm here, and not to be feared. The levels of security are different from other places, but overall, Panama is very safe. Does crime happen here? Of course it does. But, just like anywhere else, it's your responsibility to take appropriate precautions and avoid certain neighborhoods and areas. Most of the neighborhoods expats prefer in Panama do offer a gated living environment and 24-hour security.

Lifestyle

Most expats that move to Panama find that overall their daily habits are similar to wherever they came from. For those that work, you still get up and go to an office five or six days a week. However, perhaps you want to relax on the weekends by exploring the two oceans now within an easy drive from your front door. (The Pacific coast beaches can be reached in about an hour from the city, and the Caribbean side in about two hours.)

Water is safe to drink from the tap (in the city). You'll shop for your food at a supermarket when you live in the city. The roadway infrastructure as a whole is much more sophisticated than anywhere else in Central America. Most condominium buildings (and many homes) come with swimming pools. Shopping options include the choice of nine malls in and around the city. Much of the day-to-day life is the same as in other places, and these things add up to an attractive offering for many people.

The Dining Scene

Eating out in Panama is less expensive than most cities in the U.S. and Europe, so for some people, that option adds a nice differential to their lifestyle. Because of the confluence of cultures that the Panama Canal has brought to this tiny country in the past 100 years, a plethora of dining options exist, from super casual to really nice. Dining out in Panama is also one of the highlights of the local social scene. Read more on restaurants in the city in Chapter 13.

Pace

Get used to standing in line

With the Atlantic Ocean on the north side of the country, Panama has had significant Caribbean influence over the years. The culture shows this. The pace of life is much slower than in developed nations. It's even slower than other Latin American countries, according to my expat friends who've lived in them. Processes are much slower. Things take much longer. This is often a big cultural adjustment for most expats, but with time, they learn how to accommodate for it.

Is Panama right for you?

There are many, many things to consider when you're evaluating Panama as a potential place to live. It's an interesting, unique little place, which has a lot to offer. But it's not for everyone. Much of your success in finding your new life in Panama has to do with managing your expectations about your life here. (For more on forming realistic expectations as a new expat in Panama, refer to my first book.)

3

WHY PANAMA MAKES SENSE FOR MANY RETIREES

(AND THOSE SEEKING A MORE RELAXED LIFESTYLE)

Fresh fare at a roadside stand

MANY BABY BOOMERS from Westernized countries are looking at Panama as an affordable place to retire. Panama has a lot of benefits for retirees. In fact, the Panama Jubilado (or Pensionado) Visa has been rated one of the top in the world. Add that to many of the rankings Panama continues to get, including those naming

Panama as one of the top places in the world to retire (including a recent one by U.S. News and World Report) and it's hard not to give Panama some serious consideration.

Interestingly enough, there's beginning to be a trend of those younger than retirement age – think late 30's, 40's and 50's – coming to Panama in search of a more relaxed lifestyle. And, there's a larger number of younger expats finding their way to Panama. (For details on YEP!, the Young Expats in Panama group, see the interview with their founder, Skyler Ralston, in Chapter 10.) And for Panama's popular Pensionado visa, there's actually no age restriction. You can get that visa at any age as long as you show a regular pension income.

Before we get into specifics of the retirement visa, here are some of the attributes Panama has that so many Baby Boomers find attractive.

- The U.S. dollar is the currency, so for U.S. expats, there's no hassle of exchange.
- Panama has a tropical environment. It's only 500 miles North of the equator, and it's the type of climate many expats have envisioned for themselves when they retire.
- Cost of living can be affordable. It's not cheap, but it can be affordable. (For more on this, read Chapter 7 of the first in the series of the Gringo Guide to Panama.) In some areas, it can cost less to live in Panama than in the U.S.
- Panama supposedly has around 50,000 U.S. expats living in the country (though not necessarily all retired). What does that mean for you? It means you'll

have the opportunity to discover new friendships and connections within that community.

- Let me be clear that there are no retirement *villages* in Panama; that development concept has not made it here yet. Retirees to Panama often find Coronado more comfortable because there's a large number of other retired expats living in that area. Boquete (in the Interior of the country in the mountains) is also very attractive to this crowd.

- Sophisticated medical services are available in Panama, as you will read in Chapter 8. The further out you live from Panama City, the less sophisticated the medical services become. It's important to consider this if you have medical needs that need frequent attention. (I suggest that you take a tour of the private hospitals when you visit Panama (before you move) to get a realistic picture of what you can expect.)

- Panama has so many modern amenities that there will be moments that you look around and think, "Where am I? Isn't this supposed to be a 'developing nation'?" And, it is. Yes, there are two new Starbucks as of late 2015, and all kinds of franchised restaurants from the U.S. in the city. But Toto, even with all of this glitz and glam, it's important you realize, there are still aspects of this country that will make you wish for the ease of living back in Kansas, every once in a while.

Panama's Acclaimed Retirement Visa

The Pensionado Visa is a visa that anyone over the age of 18 can apply for and receive with valid, recurring monthly pension payments. You will need an attorney in Panama to take you through the process, as it's complicated and can take up to two years to get the visa. (For more on the importance of having an attorney in Panama, refer to Chapter 12 of the first book in the Gringo Guide to Panama series).

The great news is that once you receive the Pensionado Visa, you have it for life. Here are some of the benefits this visa provides for you when you retire in Panama.

- Duty-free car imports and car purchases (every two years)
- Duty-free importation of household goods worth up to $10,000 (one-time)
- In-country discounts including:
  - 25% off domestic flights
  - 25% off restaurant bills
  - 15% off hospital services
  - 25% off water and electricity bills
  - 10% off prescription drugs
  - 50% off public events
  - And more

Important: When you are approved for the *Pensionado* visa in Panama, you are not legally allowed to work or be employed elsewhere within the country. This visa was created as a benefit for those that are *truly* retired. Please check with your attorney for details on this restriction if this is a concern for you.

Building Your Social Network

If you're thinking about retiring in Panama, it's important to give some serious thought to how you will connect with other people to establish your social network. These are probably the most common questions I hear from retirement age women: How will I find friends? How will I connect with other people, so that I am not isolated and alone?

Your social network is where everything else about your life intersects: your language abilities, your mobility, your health, and your access to activities outside your home (church, club, association, etc.).

If you live in an area already known for expats, like the Coronado beach area on the Pacific side, or in Boquete or El Valle, one of the little mountain towns, you will be much more likely to run into other retirement-age expats in your day-to-day life. These areas are small and have a larger population of expats than other areas in Panama.

If you live in the city of Panama, it may be much harder to find ways to connect, because of the city's size. And, unfortunately, the resources for retirement-age folk in the city are **no different** than those the rest of us have. (I talk more on the general topic of making friends in general in the first book.)

Volunteering

In other countries, where a lot of cultural activities exist – like museums and clubs – some retirees find ample opportunities to volunteer and get involved. In Panama, these volunteer opportunities are not as easy to find. It's not as simple as getting in your car and driving to the local library, for example, without dealing with significant traffic and parking challenges, at least if you're located in the city. Otherwise, maybe a dozen museums even exist *in the entire country* and again, volunteer opportunities may require Spanish speaking skills.

Again, locate and talk to your fellow expats. They may be aware of local foundations or groups that could take advantage of your talents and expertise. A local introduction is the best way to find an inside track to somewhere that you can contribute.

Do your homework

If you have a language barrier, unless you choose to live in an area where there are a lot of other English speakers, living in Panama as a retired person can feel lonely and disconnected according to many other retired-age expats I've spoken with.

It's important to really consider what you want your lifestyle to look like in Panama *before you move*. I don't say these things to discourage you, but I hear this complaint all the time and it's disheartening. Many retirement aged people that came to Panama with unrealistic ideas about what their lives would be end up returning to their home country after a year or two, because they could not find a solid social support base.

We're all fortunate to have the beauty of the social media network in the world today. Use Facebook, Google+, and online blogs so that you can talk directly with other retirement age expats about the experiences they've had in Panama.

But whatever you decide, I do urge you to please do your homework. Remember that only you can decide if Panama is really right for you.

4

HEALTHCARE SYSTEMS IN PANAMA

Paitilla Medical Center: A favorite with expats

Quality of Care and Access

When you read about Panama, one of the advantages that's usually mentioned is the affordable healthcare system. The second thing that's mentioned is the affiliation that Punta Pacifica Hospital (in the city) has with the Johns Hopkins medical system.

The level of care available in Panama is not necessarily the same as you will find in the U.S. or Canada, though we do enjoy access to physicians and pharmaceuticals here that aren't always available in other Central American countries.

Are there a wide range of physicians in Panama? Yes. Can you find pretty much every type of care you would expect to in a Westernized medical system? Yes. The providers one might need for day-to-day, preventive care are generally available. However, if you have a very specialized need, you'll want to do some research before you move.

We had our ups and downs with the access to the healthcare that exists in Panama. Generally, it was more positive than negative.

There are a number of good private hospitals in Panama. Doctor and dentist visits are about half of what they might cost in the States. Related tests like X-rays are considerably less expensive – consider $25-50, versus $300-400 you might be charged in any U.S. city. (Refer to Chapter 7 in the first Gringo Guide to Panama book for more details on the overall cost of living in Panama.)

Prescriptions are pretty easy to get here, though the availability of some types depends on that drug's classification. Some medications (like Class II narcotics) cannot be prescribed by a Panamanian doctor unless the patient is physically admitted to a hospital. Others, however, like birth control, can be purchased without a prescription for cash at any pharmacy. If you are considering a move to Panama, you should check into the availability of any meds you regularly take, so that you know what steps will be necessary to get them once you live here.

Pharmacies can be found in most every town and city in the country, though they may look a bit less sophisticated than your average Walgreens up North. Many local pharmacies do not maintain consistent inventories of medications. This lack of inventory can require a visit to two or three pharmacies to get everything you may need.

How to Find a Good Doctor

Sufficient health care is available in Panama, as I've said. It is simply a matter of educating yourself on where to look to find the providers that work for you. The best care you'll find is in the city (Panama) because that's where the greatest density of the country's population lives.

However, even in the Interior (west of the city), you'll find clinics, hospitals and physicians who can provide you with good basic care. For more serious ailments, expats that live in the Interior may find themselves traveling back to the city on a regular basis to take advantage of the more sophisticated hospital systems that exist there.

Stepping back in Time

As you've probably read elsewhere, medical costs in Panama are lower than in the U.S. or Canada, hands down. However, the medical systems and processes are also not always as sophisticated as those countries. Walking into a doctor's office in Panama may feel like you are stepping back a few years when you end up waiting for a long time to actually see the doctor. Or when you go in for your exam and see that the equipment in his/her office is manual versus electronic.

Think 1950's-1960's in the States, when doctors were considered to be gods and their patients did exactly what they said without a lot of questions. That's still the pervading attitude among doctors in Panama today, especially when you are seen by a physician over the age of 50.

Now, just because this God complex exists doesn't mean you can't ask questions of your medical professional. In fact, you can and you should. But, it can be frustrating to encounter attitudes and egos that accompany this state of how medicine is practiced in the country.

In the past few years, however, new hospitals have begun construction and/or opened in parts of the Interior. If you are considering a move to a less populated area, you will want to check the status of the nearest hospital to you in advance to know exactly what they can provide for you, and what they can't.

The local doctor is still largely seen as knowing all, and the patient is expected to take the doctor's advice and do it. (As the majority of physicians in Panama are still male, some of this may also be due to the Latin *machismo*.) Needless to say, coming from a more sophisticated medical culture like the U.S. where the burden of education lies with the patient, this attitude can be unsettling and uncomfortable.

Observed Cultural Differences
My husband was seeing a specialist with an office at Punta Pacifica Hospital (the Johns Hopkins affiliate in the city).

He had several appointments over a few weeks. Every time he went to an appointment, he waited up to two hours to see the physician! And that was with an appointment!

He spoke to the physician on the second visit about his tardiness after waiting two hours, and asked why this was happening. The doctor made excuses that were not logical, and said it would not happen again. But on the third appointment, after 45 minutes past the hour, my husband got fed up and simply left.

There were no apologies, no explanations and no follow-up from the doctor or his office after this – not even a phone call to inquire why my husband did not return! Nothing. Needless to say, he changed doctors and never went back.

Here's another example. I had to see a cardiologist in our second year here. I got a recommendation to one of the top ones in the country. My first appointment included a number of tests, which the doctor himself performed. For an echocardiogram, the exam required that I wear a gown that opened to the front so that some wires could be attached to my chest.

When the doctor asked me to climb up onto the table for the exam, he told me to lay on my left side and give him '*my best Sports Illustrated swimsuit edition pose*' and laughed. Then he continued on to tell me that this was the advice he gave all his patients, when they came in for this particular exam and had to 'get up on the table'.

I think I laughed nervously at the time, because his comments caught me so off guard. I was already nervous and in an extremely vulnerable state of undress in my exam robe, worried about what the results of this test could mean. The appropriateness of his comments did not really process until later.

But later on, I wondered: *Did he **really** just say that to me in a medical setting? Where the heck was his professionalism? Is he even allowed to say that?*

Now, for a few uptight, stick-up-the-spine North Americans, a comment like that from a doctor to a patient could easily lead to a filed complaint, a slap on the wrist, or even a law suit for ill-timed, unprofessional behavior, and perhaps even sexual overtures.

Guess what? For many patients in Panama, that kind of thing may not even raise an eyebrow. The sensitivity to sexual undertones is extremely low in a country where *machismo* still largely rules society.

Did I personally find the comment appropriate? Of course not, but in some way, the doctor seemed to be trying to put me at ease. His cultural background made it acceptable to attempt to do so with this type of conversation. (I suppose my cultural background is a bit more reserved, to say the least.)

Meanwhile, the story has made for good dinner conversation over the years.

On another occasion, I made an appointment with a renowned dermatologist. I checked in on time for the appointment when I arrived. After 45 minutes, I was told it would be at least another hour before the doctor would see me.

When I inquired about the hold-up, the young women at the front desk were apoplectic. After giving the front desk an earful on my understanding of what it meant to have an appointment (which did not help advance my cause), I left and never went back. As you can imagine, I was incredulous at how rude this was. I kept thinking: *It wasn't as if the woman was delivering babies, for God's sake! She is a frickin' dermatologist!*

Again, no phone call from the office. No follow-up, and no apologies.

These stories begin to give you a clear picture of how one can easily get frustrated with the medical system's inefficiencies.

While these examples don't mean that this will be what you will experience with every physician you encounter, it's safe to assume you'll experience some marked cultural differences.

The level of medical professionalism will often be lower or at least noticeably *different*, both with the doctors themselves and their staff.

Continuing Education for Doctors

A few other things to keep in mind as it relates to the medical services in Panama: while many of the local physicians graduate from medical school in the States, the local licensing in Panama does not require them to do ongoing training every few years in order to maintain their medical license.

As a result, many of the philosophies and treatments locally may be based on knowledge acquired some years ago, versus the latest information and research. This is not necessarily a bad thing, but it's something to keep in mind, because it will have an impact on the routes they recommend to you for your treatment and follow-up.

Also, you can't expect that the support staff in the clinics and hospitals will speak English. In fact, you shouldn't because they generally don't. Keep that in mind, as you attempt to navigate the system locally. Making appointments, following up on test results, and dealing with insurance providers can be very frustrating when you can't speak the language.

If you are not at least partially fluent or just prefer to be very clear in your communication, take a fellow Spanish-speaking expat or friend with you to your appointments. It's better to do that than to take the risk of not understanding something correctly, especially when it comes to something as important as your health.

(For more on the importance of learning Spanish, read Chapter 3 of the first Gringo Guide to Panama book.)

General Practitioners

In the U.S. and Canada, when you get sick, you're likely to pick up the phone and make an appointment with your family doctor or an internist to see what's going on with your health. If your illness is non-specific, like a flu, a sprain, or an ache, an appointment with a doctor that has a general practice is probably where you would start. If things develop further, you might make a second appointment with a specialist.

In Panama, there's not a wealth of general practitioner physicians. It's not clear why this is the case, but it's not easy to locate and find a general doctor here as it is in the States.

I have yet to find a general doctor that I can call for just any old health ailment question. I still find this frustrating. Back home, I had two or three doctors that I had on speed dial. These were people I had built relationships with over the years. My husband, on the other hand, did find a general practitioner (by recommendation from a fellow male expat) and has been very happy with him.

After you move, you will quickly realize the value of your past connections and the comfort they brought you, as you find yourself starting over from scratch. If you moved to Panama to work for an embassy, you will be fortunate to have the support of embassy-identified medical professionals for your family's health care needs.

It may be that the low number of general doctors in Panama is specific to the fact that one can make a lot more money as a specialist. Certainly it's common knowledge that brain surgeons make more than family doctors. These days with socialized medicine being (or becoming) the norm in many countries, doctors don't make the money they used to (at least in the U.S.).

The very best way to find a doctor is to ask your expat friends and colleagues for personal recommendations. Some doctors in Panama cater specifically to the expat population.

If you move here and don't have any local connections (yet), you can find some of these same doctors advertising in the English-speaking local publications. (Yes, it is a little strange to see a doctor advertise.) Schedule a get-to-know-you appointment, and while there, ask for any references they can provide who will be willing to talk to you about the care they have received from a patient's point of view.

Obstetrics and Gynecology Care

One of my biggest worries when we relocated to Panama was finding a doctor I could trust to take care of my female needs. I personally was past childbearing age when we moved to Panama, so I was not concerned about the obstetrical side of medical care. However, as I did my research, and saw several gynecologists over the first three years of our life in Panama, I did find that most gynecologists also practice obstetrics. Babies are big business in Latin America with so much of the continent being Catholic, so if you are in this phase of your life, you'll easily be able to find a doctor in the country.

Because finding the right gynecological care is such a personal decision, I had a number of appointments (and some not-so-great experiences) before I found the doctor with whom I currently work.

I asked all my expat friends and my lady colleagues at work to give me their recommendations. No different than anything else, even these personal recommendations for gynecologists varied widely. But, for being new to town, personal recommendations are the best place to start.

I also consulted the phone book. But, unless you speak Spanish, the phone book (or the online directory at http://www.PaginasAmarillas.com) is not all that useful.

The hardest thing for me in this department was feeling comfortable with a doctor who only spoke limited English. Discussing one's most sensitive healthcare needs is hardly ideal when there's even a small language barrier. Because of this, I maintained a relationship with my gynecologist in the States the entire time I lived in Panama, so that I could easily get a second opinion if I needed one.

The process of finding the gynecologist I used in Panama took me to five different clinics.

I didn't like the first one's office – it felt outdated and old to me, and the guy's English was stilted, so I wasn't sure we were really communicating all that well.

The second doctor I went to was a well-known female physician – very famous locally – but her bedside approach was more brusque, and her exam more uncomfortable than any male doctor I'd ever seen. Needless to say, I didn't go back.

The third doctor recommended an emergency surgery to remedy a minor problem he found. He scared me so badly that I took his advice without seeking a second opinion, and then later found out that the surgery really hadn't been necessary, according to my gynecologist in the States. Whether he was giving me outdated advice or was fleecing me (as the surgery was close to $1,000 even after my health insurance paid), it's hard to say. But, either way it was not a good feeling to learn I'd taken a recommendation, which wasn't in my best interest.

I tried three times to schedule with the fourth doctor, but was never successful. She must be pretty good because her schedule is always booked months in advance, but I finally gave up trying to make an appointment.

The fifth office was the one I selected – a Colombian physician with a reserved manner who speaks solid English.

Alternative Medicine

For many years prior to moving to Panama, I utilized a number of alternative medicine healthcare providers in the States. I regularly partook of such practices as acupuncture, chiropractic care, and homeopathic medicine as part of my healthcare routine. In fact, I had such good success with these practitioners that I often visited them first for an ailment before seeing my doctor who practiced Western medicine.

Unfortunately in Panama, alternative medicine is only now being discovered and beginning to be appreciated, and it's fledging at best. I just recently saw a Bach Flower remedies practitioner advertise in the classifieds in *The Visitor*, but that's the only one I've heard of since we've lived here. While a small number of chiropractors do practice in the city, most of them employ older styles, which I found to be less gentle. I was thrilled in 2015 to discover a clinic run by an American in Punta Paitilla (in the city) that utilizes more up-to-date methods. During my time in Panama, I only discovered two acupuncturists in the city (neither of which I can recommend) and one homeopathist (who is from Colombia and is amazing). The alternative medical industry as a whole locally appears to be relatively unsophisticated and certainly, less regulated than the one that exists in the U.S.

A limited number of U.S. physicians in these fields practice illegally in the country, providing care to expats who seek them out. I've heard of a chiropractor – supposedly quite good – in Coronado, an acupuncturist in San Francisco (trained in New York), and a general practitioner in El Valle that fall into this category.

I say they are illegal because if you were a doctor in another country and you move to Panama, you have to shadow a Panamanian doctor for two years locally before you can apply for a medical license. This is a protective measure by the government to ensure that local doctors have a leg up in the field. Few foreign doctors decide to go this route, for obvious reasons. As a result, some foreign retired doctors have begun an underground business in the areas where they live.

I don't promote this activity, but on the other hand, if you find them experienced enough to provide you with the medical advice that you need, then that is completely your call.

Generally, one should anticipate that the availability of alternative medical care in the country is slim to none. This was good news for the providers I use in the States, as it meant I was still patronizing their clinics on our return visits even while we lived in Panama.

Dental Care

The availability of affordable dental care is quite good in Panama. At the recommendation of another expat friend, we found a good dentist group in our first few months here, and I was a patient at that clinic the entire time I lived there.

The dentists at this particular clinic are trained in Panama, though some studied abroad. As a result, some speak English and some do not. This clinic, like a number of others in the city, offers the entire range of dental and orthodontic services one might find anywhere including fillings, braces, implants, mouthpieces, and surgery.

Costs are approximately half of what you can find in the U.S. at some clinics. With our particular doctor, we started out paying about ⅓ of what we might have with our dentists in the States, but now we're paying about ⅔, so his fees have increased over the past few years. (As an example, I paid $50 in December 2015 for my annual cleaning.)

A growing number of foreigners are coming to Panama in search of more affordable dental care, and they are finding it. Evidently, there are even some insurance plans in the U.S. that will pay for dental procedures done in Panama. To find out if yours offers this option, contact your insurance provider directly.

Once again, to find a dentist or oral surgeon that's right for you, ask for recommendations. I personally don't trust ads, though you will see a number of clinics promoting themselves in the tourist and hotel magazines.

The Real Life Litmus Test of the Urgent Care System: My encounter with a scorpion

As you will read in a future chapter, scorpions are more common in Panama during the summer months of December through May, when the climate is somewhat drier and much hotter. In fact, I only saw half a dozen of these little devils in eight years.

However, on one particular Saturday morning, I encountered the fourth one in a not so very pleasant way. I moved a bag, which my crustacean friend was living under, and he backed into my hand about the same time I saw him. He struck and I screamed. And, I can tell you that the sting of a scorpion hurts in a very big way. Badly.

Imagine the things that ran through my head: I'd heard as a child the things that happen to your body when you get stung by a scorpion. I had heard once that you would probably die if a scorpion stung you. And that it hurt like heck. (And, the latter one was correct; it did.) Likely these stories in my head were helped along by a Western movie or two from the 60s and 70s.

At any rate, our weekend home where this happened is minutes from the nearest urgent care clinic in Coronado, on the Pacific coast. Needless to say, we were gathered up and on our way there within three minutes after I got stung.

On the way there – my husband drove – and I cried. The pain was steady but my hand was swelling to almost twice its normal size. The rapid swelling caused as much pain as the sting itself.

When we arrived at the clinic, it was 10 AM on Saturday morning. There was no one even waiting in the waiting room. We walked straight in and I announced to the front desk what had happened. The guy sitting there spoke perfect English to us. He took us back to see the doctor immediately.

Within moments, a nurse was taking my blood pressure and the attending doctor came to the room. He asked a few questions, while my husband filled out the forms for our local insurance with the front desk person.

Within five minutes of our arrival, my blood had been drawn. The blood test would verify if the scorpion was venomous or not. I was then moved to another area for an IV to administer an anti-venom, anti-allergen medicine concoction.

All in all, the exam and treatment took an hour top to bottom. This included a thorough review of my blood test results with the doctor before I left, as well as me receiving a copy of the results for my records. He also wrote a prescription in case I had any lingering side effects in the ensuing day or two. (Happily, the blood test came back negative for venom, which was a huge relief.)

While the sting area had doubled in size within ten minutes from the time I got stung, that initial swelling was reduced to almost nothing within the hour I had the IV treatment. The pain medication included in the IV started working within five minutes of the IV too, which was also a huge relief.

What was the total bill for my scorpion sting? Zero. I paid absolutely nothing out of pocket. As it was an accident (obviously), my insurance paid everything from the get go. Other than some significant pain for about six hours after the sting, I had a great experience with the responsiveness of the local medical system.

This was by far the most positive experience I had with the medical system in Panama. I can't tell you how grateful we were for the blessing of easy access to a very professional, clean, efficient clinic close to where we lived. On-call doctors. Zero cost. And, most of all, they knew exactly what to do for my ailment. It was a very reassuring experience.

Soon after, I called the exterminator to come and spray the house in order to encourage my little scorpion neighbors to depart the premises. That was the doctor's final recommendation, and you better believe, I took it.

Surgery in Panama: Our Personal Story

My husband and I were fortunate. We both had local medical insurance through Pan-American Life in Panama. Health insurance in Panama functions in a similar fashion to what health insurance in the 1980s did in the U.S. When you visit the doctor, you have a set co-pay amount. In our case, the copay was $8 to $12 for a general doctor visit, if the provider was on the approved insurance list. After that, for anything that happened, we were responsible for 20% and the insurance company covered 80%. Emergencies were covered 100%, thankfully.

When you go to the lab to have something done – an Xray or bloodwork – you have to pay for it. Then comes the lovely process of getting reimbursed. Again, think 1980s: paperwork, paperwork and a lengthy period of waiting. I am still not aware at this writing of any insurance company in Panama providing online tracking for your claims, either. The tracking system is up to you. Reimbursement checks can take from three to eight weeks.

In early 2012, my husband needed to have surgery. This was the first time we needed to use our Panama health insurance for something major. We decided to compare apples to apples, between him electing to have the surgery in Panama versus doing it back in the U.S.

Identifying your Surgeon

Our first line of thinking was to find a doctor who had the relevant experience in this type of surgery. Hubby got two referrals from his regular doctor and went and spoke to both. He then went to see a doctor he used to see in the U.S. that he knew and trusted. After speaking to all three about their experience, how many procedures they had done in the last year, and success rates, he felt comfortable in deciding to have the surgery in Panama.

The selected local surgeon filled out all the papers needed with our insurance company for my husband's surgery pre-authorization. (The insurance company will tell you the preauthorization takes 2-4 business days, but that's not reality. Ours took three weeks.)

Medical Costs Breakdown

Though we ultimately elected to have the surgery in Panama, part of our consideration once we determined that the quality of care was sufficient was analyzing the cost differences. Here's a recap of the insurance costs breakdown, and how it compared if the procedure was done locally in or in the U.S.

Procedure done in Panama in 2012:

Surgery cost of $3,730 – Note that this was the amount that the insurance authorized. The surgeon's office said that without the pre-authorization, the cost of the surgery would be closer to $5,500. I was anticipating this to be a 80/20 kind of split, after the $75 copay. Since the type of surgery my husband had falls under outpatient surgery, we were told we would only need to pay the copay on the day of the procedure, and the insurance would cover the rest.

Procedure done in the U.S.:

Our PanAmerican Life health insurance in Panama had a $1,000 deductible for any procedure done in the U.S. The quote for the same surgery with my husband's trusted orthopedic surgeon back home in Denver came in at $10,700. Less the deductible, that left $9,700. The insurance then had a ceiling of $5,000 for any covered procedure conducted in the U.S. So, from the $9,700 remaining, deduct $5,000, and that leaves a balance of $4,700. Total cost to us if the procedure was done in the U.S.: $5,700.

Now, remember for the U.S. part, this was pure medical costs for the surgery. It did not include travel expenses. Nor, did either of these cover the ensuing physical therapy visits which were necessary in the weeks that followed.

The Bottom Line

We found a competent, experienced orthopedic surgeon in Panama, and we saved a ton of money due to our insurance coverage. And even if we had not had the insurance, the retail cost for the surgery in Panama would have been $5,200 less than if the surgery had been performed in the U.S.

Note: Physical therapy sessions in Panama cost about half what they would have in the U.S.. Happily, a U.S.-trained physical therapist was located here in Panama with whom my husband felt very comfortable. Four months of weekly therapy cost around $850 out of pocket. Insurance did reimburse me for 60% of these costs after the fact.

Is price the only consideration?

Now, health care is not something you want to skimp on. These are not decisions where you want to always go for the lowest price, especially when it's a major thing like surgery.

My recommendation on looking at something like this in Panama is to always do your homework – on the providers, on how many procedures they've done, considering referrals of other expats who have had experiences with that same professional, etc. You can't be too careful. We were initially pleased that the research we did resulted in some significant financial savings to us.

Panama really is becoming a growing choice for expats seeking more affordable medical care. We felt fortunate that we had competent, U.S.-trained medical professionals at our fingertips, since we lived in the city. But, even so, the surgery in Panama, though it cost less, did not go as smoothly as we'd hoped.

Lessons Learned from the Surgery Experience

The previous paragraphs focused on the analysis we went through related to choosing the right physician, and weighing the surgery costs. It's important to share other pertinent details that had a big impact on the overall experience.

On the day of the surgery, we arrived early – 7:30 AM, as scheduled at the hospital. My husband had to fast – not even a drop of water allowed that morning – so in the spirit of moral support, I fasted with him.

Admissions at the hospital

Check-in at the hospital took an hour. The waiting wasn't like many of the take-a-number-at-the-meat-counter experiences I've had in most other *locales* here, thankfully. But, four families arrived simultaneously, and two waited in a small waiting area, while the other two did their paperwork in small glassed-in rooms. The attendants did not speak English. (Refer to Chapter 3 of the first book in the Gringo Guide to Panama series on the reality of language here in Panama.)

Lesson Learned #1: If you are having surgery, the person that goes with you on the day of surgery should bring their cell phone and their identification with them. The hospital will ask you for your cell number, and make a copy of your ID. Assumedly, this is so they can get in touch with you if something goes wrong.

Once we checked in, we were directed to the emergency room waiting area. My husband was taken to be prepped for the surgery. I was summoned after a few minutes to verify something with the nurse because she did not speak English, and my husband's Spanish is stilted.

At 8:45 AM, another aide came to take my husband into surgery. I was directed to another waiting room in the main part of the hospital. We had yet to see the doctor – even to be greeted, though this is not unusual at this point in time, even in the States.

I asked the aide when we would see the doctor. He told me that the doctor would come see me in the waiting area right before he went in to start the surgery. My husband was wheeled in to the surgery area without me.

I dutifully arranged myself in the waiting room. Two other families were already there. The clock read 9 AM. The surgery was originally scheduled to start at 9 AM. Thankfully, I had brought my own water, Gatorade and snacks. (I learned long ago in Panama that you're pretty much on your own much of the time in finding healthy snacks, so you better plan ahead.)

The waiting room was clean and the décor included high-top tables, as well as couches and chairs. A sign advertised Free Wifi. (I did have my laptop, so I was happy to see that.) Unfortunately, there was a required password for the Wifi, and no one around to ask for it! When I did finally find someone to request it, they only spoke Spanish.

A small bathroom off the waiting area was conveniently located, and a water cooler (with cups!) was also there, as well as several magazines and newspapers. (The experience up to this point had been so smooth that I almost felt like I was back in the States for a moment, except the TV was blaring an annoying Spanish-speaking show, instead of Oprah or Dr. Oz.)

The waiting area

Thirsty, I went to the cooler for some water....and found the bottle was empty. I looked around for a vending machine, but there was nothing in sight. I was afraid to leave the waiting room, since I'd been told the doctor would come out to see me prior to starting surgery.

The minutes ticked by, mostly in time with my stomach rumbling. The clock registered 9:30 AM. Since we rose at 6 AM, and I still hadn't eaten breakfast, I was getting grouchy. Naturally there was no hospital aide around to advise on where I could get a bite to eat.

More time went by and not a doctor in sight. I waited, and waited some more. Bottom line, he never came out to see me before the surgery. What we had been told was either incorrect or he forgot. So I never got a recap of what to expect until *after* the surgery was over. This was not only annoying, but I also thought it was pretty rude. The lack of any words of reassurance from the physician who would be cutting on my husband *prior* to the surgery did not help my frame of mind at all.

Lesson Learned #2: Whatever specific questions you have about the surgery need to be written down and asked at the *last office visit prior to the surgery* – NOT when you get to the hospital. Because there's a good chance your doctor won't show up to talk to you prior to the surgery either.

Because I'm familiar with the area around the hospital, I walked down the street (finally having given up on the doctor coming out to speak to me) to a nearby coffee shop and bakery.

Surgery was scheduled to take two hours. It ended up taking two and a half. Then, there's the post-op recovery. (We'd been told nothing about what this might look like in advance.)

Hubby was brought out of La La land, waited for probably 30 minutes, then was taken back to the place where he'd originally disrobed to be re-dressed in his street clothes, since the procedure was outpatient surgery.

Meanwhile, two doctors came to see me in the main waiting room. The anesthesiologist also came out. All three told me that the surgery had gone very well. They described what they had done – in Spanish first, and then in English to be sure I fully understood. (When I recounted what they said to my husband later, I realized I should have made some quick notes while I was speaking to them. I'm not fluent in medical terms, so I got most of it, but with the stress of the day, my memory was not perfect after the fact.)

The anesthesiologist brought out two prescriptions. He explained there were two pain medications. The expected stuff – anti-inflammatory, antibiotics and one pain medicine – were on one prescription pad. The other prescription with the second pain medicine – a narcotic – was written on a sheet by itself.

This second prescription was the heavy-duty stuff, which in Panama is considered a Class II narcotic. (What we've learned is that you must be physically in the hospital (and usually admitted or having had surgery) to get this prescription. Only an anesthesiologist can prescribe Class II narcotics.)

The hospital pharmacy

While my husband was being re-dressed, I took the prescriptions to the hospital pharmacy (in the same building) to be filled. This took two trips, because the first time, the gal there misread the pain medication dosage and told me they did not have that dosage. This required me returning to the waiting area, finding the hospital aide, and having her call the anesthesiologist to ask him about changing it.

Naturally, by then, the anesthesiologist had left the hospital, so we were going to be in a world of trouble until I realized that the aide had misread the prescription. I hurried back to the pharmacy and once I pointed out the error in how they had read the prescription, they were able to fill it. (Again, it's a good thing I speak Spanish.)

Lesson Learned #3: When you meet the anesthesiologist soon after check-in and before the surgery commences, ask him or her for the prescriptions at that time. You can then go fill them while the surgery is happening, to save time, and allay any issues versus having to do this while your loved one is in recovery.

Unfortunately, while the hospital aide and I were doing all of this, my husband was sitting in intense pain in the post-surgery room. When he told me that he had not been given *any* pain medication after the surgery, we immediately consulted the aide.

The aide made some calls but then told us, *'Sorry, once the patient exits the surgical suite, the hospital can't give him anything else. You have to ask for that before you get to this point.'* My response to that was *'What? My husband is still out of it. How is he supposed to know to ask for that? He's barely even able to communicate!'*

The bottom line was that nothing could be done, and my husband had to wait for me to come back with the prescriptions, and then take a pill, which took 30-45 minutes to kick in. This was a very unpleasant experience for him.

Lesson Learned #4: At that point, I should have called the anesthesiologist immediately – he had given me his card. Add this to your pre-surgery list of questions: *What type of pain medication is administered after the surgery but before I leave the hospital, so that I am comfortable until I get home and can get my other prescriptions?*

Pay before you can leave

In departing the hospital, I was asked to settle up on the financial account before we were allowed to leave.

Evidently, this is common here, as it must be hard to collect debts once people have left, since there's no useful mail system. Unfortunately, this entailed my husband sitting in a wheelchair in the emergency room hallway, and me standing beside him for almost 30 minutes, until the woman behind the payment window called our name. This was incredibly painful for him, again just fresh out of recovery with the anesthesia wearing off.

Finally, once we had settled up, the hospital attendant disappeared – meaning once the bill was paid, I had to push the wheelchair out to the car myself, and get my 200 lb.+ husband into our SUV. Not an easy task to say the least.

Lesson Learned #5: Ask for someone to assist you in this, because depending on where you are parked – it could mean otherwise that your patient will sit by himself in the hall, while you go get the car, bring it up, and then navigate the wheelchair and unloading process over some bumps in the emergency entrance. (Don't assume it's all smooth concrete, because while this particular one was better than most out-door areas in Panama, it still wasn't great.)

More in the Days that Followed

The doctor never called to check in that night to see how my husband was doing, nor did he do so in the days that followed. (This would be a norm in the U.S. and one that we as Gringos take very much for granted.)

With five different medications – including two for pain – we weren't entirely clear once we got home about how the two pain medications interacted. The way I recalled they had been explained to me by the anesthesiologist did not make sense after the fact.

We ended up administering them in the way I recalled, until Day 3. However, my husband was still having a lot of pain. On the evening of Day 3, my husband finally threw in the towel and reverted to using pain meds he had from another earlier U.S. prescription. I'm still grateful that he had that old prescription in the cabinet, because it made a big difference for him.

I can't tell you how thankful I was for Google during the post-surgery days. We all take for granted the easy technology we enjoy at our fingertips every day, but it really can be a lifesaver. An easy search helped me find and review the potential interactions of the different prescriptions, as none of that was explained to me at the time the doctor gave me the prescriptions. Nor did I think to ask about it either, as stressed as I was at the time.

It's important to note that Panama does **not** require that this type of written information (about the drug, its side effects, and possible interactions) accompany the filled prescriptions. While there is some type of a drug administration entity in Panama, their requirements are not the same as those of the Food & Drug Administration in the U.S. So, be sure to ask your physician about this in an earlier appointment, or at the time you receive the written prescriptions.

The first follow-up appointment was five days later in the doctor's office. (At which, my husband was made to wait an hour, which was extremely uncomfortable.)

Post-Surgery Therapeutic Support

The brace my husband was given at the hospital – and told to wear 24/7 for the first few weeks – was flimsy and did not provide enough support for him in his post-surgery condition.

This led to me doing a whirlwind tour of four different Arrocha (the equivalent of a Walgreens or Boots), one Metro (another drug store brand), and one medical supply store in the city on Day 2 after the surgery in an effort to find another option. Unfortunately, another brand or type of brace could not be found except online, which would have taken two to three weeks to get to us in Panama. Ultimately, we returned to the States in subsequent weeks, and were able to have a better-constructed brace sent to our hotel.

Lesson Learned #6: Ask your doctor *before the surgery* what type of support or home-care products you will need afterwards. Plan to have those shipped to you, if they are not available through the physician's office or anywhere else locally, so that you have them before you have the surgery. Shipping items from the U.S. can take from two to four weeks, so plan for that as part of your timeline.

In the case of this surgery, while the surgery ultimately went well in terms of fixing what it was supposed to fix, the rest of the recovery experience was harrowing emotionally and mentally in the first few weeks after the surgery took place, due to the things I've outlined above.

While it's a fact that medical services are much less expensive in the country, I personally hesitate to promote Panama broadly as a place for medical tourism for any type of major surgery like my husband had. Much of this perspective, naturally, comes from our own experience. But, I can't help but think that ours was not necessarily unique.

Ultimately, I share these stories so that if you *do* elect to do a major surgery – even outpatient – in Panama, you won't make the same assumptions we did. I hope you can learn from our mistakes and blunders, and take these lessons toward making your own experience a smoother one.

5

PANAMA AS A LAUNCHPAD FOR TRAVEL

Tocumen International Airport

PANAMA REALLY IS the center of the Americas. If you look at the map geographically, you'll find it is literally right in the middle, joining the North and South continents. This makes Panama an ideal place for reaching all of Central and South America for travel, whether you are going for business or pleasure.

One major recommendation I make to future expats is to travel to Panama (and spend some considerable time in the country) before they select it as their new home base. In this chapter, I provide some perspective on the ease of getting in and out of Panama (especially as it relates to North America), the beauty of easy access to Latin America, and a listing of hotels in the city from a local's point of view.

In advance of booking your trip, you may wish to reference Chapter 8, which covers Panama's two seasons and climate considerations.

The City's Modern, Expanding International Airport

Tocumen International Airport in Panama City receives millions of passengers each year. And that number is growing all the time. A number of new wings inside the existing airport terminal were added since 2012. The addition of these new wings has made Tocumen easier to get in and out of, as a passenger. An entire new terminal is also under construction, with scheduled opening this year or next (2017).

Direct Flights to the U.S. and Canada
Logistically, Panama is often the connection point for flights going from North America to South America and vice versa. For those living in Panama, getting back and forth to North America – either Canada or the U.S. – is getting easier all the time.

From Tocumen, Miami and Orlando are two and a half to three hour flights. New York City (via Newark, NJ) is five hours. Dallas and Houston are four hours. Atlanta, L.A., Las

Vegas and Washington D.C. – also, all enjoy direct flights to Panama. In Canada, Toronto is also direct. Panama's own Copa Airlines has added a number of new direct flights in recent years including Boston, Denver and Tampa. You get the picture: Panama is very accessible to and from the U.S. and Canada.

For those considering retiring or working in Panama, having this great travel access makes the decision to settle here much more comfortable. If you need to return to see your kids or grandkids, you can be back in hours, or at the most, a day. Have business you need to conduct? You can work on the plane and even return that same day if you choose, especially if your destination is Orlando or Miami.

Latin America at your fingertips

Copa Airlines currently has direct flights to every single capitol city in South America. Not only do business people find this extremely convenient for reaching the markets they need to during the week – it also opens up your possibilities for exploring Latin America.

Need some inspiration for where to go? How about the volcano region in Costa Rica? It's just 1.5 hours to San Jose. Lima, Peru or Quito, Ecuador: just two hours away. Access to the cultural capitol of Bogota in Colombia: just 90 minutes away. Want to see the Amazon River in Brazil? It's just a four-hour plane ride. Interested in Easter Island off the coast of Chile? You'll jump through Santiago, Chile but can be there on the same day when you come from

Panama. Tango lessons in Buenos Aires, Argentina? They can be yours via a direct seven-hour flight.

You get the idea. Panama is a great connection point – whether you live here, work here or retire here. And if you're traveling through Tocumen International Airport, and have several hours to kill before or in between flights, you can enjoy a modern duty-free shopping area, a beautiful new food court upstairs, and even a day spa for a mani-pedi combo or a massage. As of 2013, Star Alliance members have access to the Copa Airlines lounge, which is a nice waiting area with free WiFi and snacks.

Having easy access to travel from Panama is one of the main reasons we decided to move here, and we really took advantage of it. You can too.

Where to Lay Your Head in the City

An iguana who lived in the tree next to our apartment in Amador

I remember when we came to Panama for the first time to interview in 2007. The recruiting company booked us at a staid old British hotel – aptly named The Bristol – right in the middle of the banking district downtown.

The experience was one you'd expect from a nice business-style hotel, if not a little stodgy for my particular tastes. The décor was very old-world with a lot of dark wood. However, the room was very comfortable, and a uniformed butler on the floor brought you ice when you checked in, which was kind of impressive. (The same butler returned in the evening too, for turn-down service).

The breakfast buffet included a lot of tropical fresh fruits and pastries. I found the restaurant a little small, though its chef was (and is to this day) quite acclaimed.

While the recruiting firm paid for that first trip, I did see the bill for our lodging on our second trip and the prices reflected on it shocked me. At that time, The Bristol was charging $500 a night for the room we stayed in. And that price was not for a suite or anything spectacular! What we learned is that the high prices were simply a question of supply and demand. In the city market in 2007-2008, Panama's hotel occupancy was very high (95%+) and the hotels could charge whatever the market would bear. This price gouging continued for several years in Panama to the dismay of international travelers until approximately mid 2011.

In 2009, the government offered a concession on new hotel licenses to developers who would bring hotels to the local market. Though I don't know the specifics, whatever they offered was quite attractive, because four years later, the city market was flooded with all kinds of new hotel options, which lowered price points and led to much lower occupancy.

Hotel Listings

The Radisson at the Summit in Panama

Here's a list of some of the better-known hotels in the Panama (City) market. I've added some general comments based on my own personal experiences of visiting these places – whether to see friends or colleagues staying there, from when I've eaten at the restaurants located there, or attended events in them. *(Note: if you're looking for rates for specific dates and/or detailed information on the room interiors etc., visit the specific websites for each hotel.)*

Tantalo Hotel

- Avenue B & 8th Street
- Located in Casco Viejo (the UNESCO World Heritage site area)

- Opened in early 2012
- 12 rooms
- Tasty, trendy restaurant – Tantalo Kitchen – on the main floor
- Encima, the popular rooftop bar with breathtaking views to the city skyline often features live music, DJ and special events.
- This hotel gets very *loud* on the weekends when the "In" nightlife crowd ramps up the party, so plan accordingly.
- Pricing in the $200s per room

www.tantalohotel.com

Hard Rock Hotel Megapolis
- Avenida Balboa, next to Multicentro Mall
- Located in the downtown area
- Opened in late 2012
- This is a HUGE hotel. Lots of tourists stay here.
- Direct access to MultiCentro Mall and Paitilla Hospital.
- Festive huge lobbies featuring Hard Rock shops and rock-n-roll décor.
- Seven restaurants and bars.
- Casino, day spa and beauty salon.
- From $120 or so a night

www.hrhpanamamegapolis.com

Marriott Hotel
- Located in the business district (downtown)

- Features a popular casino, as well as coffee shop, gift shop, day spa, work-out facilities and two restaurants
- This is a very large hotel and caters to loads of business travelers and tourists
- Décor is typical Marriott – a bit above a business hotel but not quite luxury
- Across the street from a popular cigar bar, which while unrelated to the hotel is locally well-known as a pick-up point for prostitutes (which by the way is legal in Panama)
- Walk-able proximity to a number of great, local restaurants
- Rates from the $200s

www.marriott.com

Hilton Garden Inn
- Opened in 2013
- In the El Cangrejo neighborhood
- Across the street from two large casinos
- Walk-able to a number of restaurants
- Typical middle-of-the-road business hotel, no frills, though it's new, nice and very clean
- Restaurant and fitness room
- Rates from the low $100s

www.hilton.com

The Bristol Hotel
- In the banking district (downtown)
- 129 rooms

- Recently renovated in 2012, which was very well done
- Very distinctive, old-world feel throughout
- Luxury service and décor
- Luxury bedding
- Workout room
- Indoor/outdoor bar on the sixth floor features nice city views
- Local, award-winning chef and restaurant
- Many business events are held at this hotel
- Rates from the $200s

www.thebristol.com

Hotel RIU

- In the banking district
- Opened in 2011
- 645 rooms
- Very large hotel catering to tourists and business travelers
- Large conference spaces for meetings and conventions
- Very funky attire in the rooms – bright colors, outlandish design, etc.
- Business center, workout room, pool
- Three restaurants
- Rates from mid $100s

www.riu.com

Le Meridien Panama

- Avenida Balboa facing the Pacific Ocean
- Opened in 2009-2010
- 111 rooms
- Upscale, very nice suites, modern design.
- Includes a Sensory Spa by Clarins
- Small conference spaces (many of the Chambers hold their monthly events here)
- Rooftop pool and lounge area
- Good ground floor restaurant
- Lobby bar has a cool vibe, which is fun for cocktails or short meetings
- Rates from $150-800

www.starwoodhotels.com

Westin Playa Bonita

- 20 minutes from downtown Panama City
- High-rise hotel facing the Pacific Ocean
- Opened in 2012
- 611 rooms
- Beautiful grounds
- Lovely pools setting
- Sensory Spa by Clarins – the nicest spa setting in the country, in my opinion
- Three restaurants
- My friends and I love to come to the Westin for a leisurely lunch and the spa
- Good people watching place

- Day passes are available for the pool and spa, which is also fun.
- *NOTE:* This hotel is really nice, but out of the way for sightseeing. If you stay here, you will likely want to rent a car or hire a regular car service. (The biggest complaint I hear from those that stay here is that getting back and forth to the city at a moment's notice is not convenient.)
- From the high $100s and up

www.starwoodhotels.com

Playa Bonita Intercontinental

Playa Bonita Intercontinental
- 20 minutes from downtown Panama
- Faces the Pacific Ocean – midrise hotel
- Rooms are all right – nothing fantastic
- Opened 15 years ago
- 332 rooms
- Vacationers and conventioners are the typical guests

- 3 restaurants – one facing the ocean, which is lovely; food is average
- Spa, lovely outdoor pools, walkable beach
- Good gift shops for unique memorabilia from Panama
- *NOTE:* This hotel is nice, but out of the way for sightseeing. If you stay here, you will likely want to rent a car or hire a regular car service. (The biggest complaint I hear from those that stay here is that getting back and forth to the city at a moment's notice is not convenient.)
- Day passes for the pool and spa are available for purchase.
- From the mid $100s

www.ihg.com

Trump Hotel

- Located in the high-end Punta Pacifica neighborhood
- The hotel is so big, you will feel like you are in your own mini-city
- Opened mid 2012
- Building also includes private condos
- 369 rooms and suites
- Gorgeous facilities, interesting room design, nice restaurants
- Great views
- Tourists, business people, high-rollng locals, some conventioners

- Very in-your-face hip, modern vibe, typical of any Trump establishment
- Five pools, with waterfront dining
- Several tasty and pricey restaurants onsite
- Cool bars for an afternoon cocktail on the 15th floor and in the casino on the 65th floor
- Lots of conferences and weddings at this venue
- Rooms from the mid $100s and up

www.trumphotelcollection.com/panama

Sheraton Hotel and Convention Center

- In the San Francisco neighborhood and across from the convention center
- Not a great area for walking around, very congested and noisy
- This hotel has been around for a while, though it recently was updated in 2012 (and they did a nice job on the common spaces)
- 369 rooms
- Lots of conferences and weddings here
- Lots of convention-goers stay here
- Very nice pool and fitness facilities
- Many locals use the Sheraton tennis club
- Three restaurants: Café Bahia downstairs has a fantastic Sunday brunch; Las Hadas on the main level is a casual, 24-hour restaurant, which is popular with locals too.
- Rates from the high $100s

www.sheratonpanama.com.pa

Waldorf Astoria

- Banking district
- Opened March 2013
- 130 rooms and suites
- Very luxurious feel
- Beautiful lobby and conference facilities
- Small spa
- Gorgeous Sunday brunch spread
- From the low $200s
- Four restaurants

www.waldorfastoriapanama.com

Las Clementinas

- Casco Viejo neighborhood (a historic UNESCO World Heritage site)
- Boutique hotel with suites
- Historic building
- Opened in 2011
- 12 rooms
- Tourists, some business people
- Each suite is a full apartment with living and dining room, kitchen, 12-foot ceilings and private balconies
- Las Clementinas Café & Bar downstairs has fantastic food and an intimate, nostalgic feel
- Great place because it's small, has good service and is walk-able to all of Casco Viejo
- Chauffeured car and custom tours available
- Featured in countless news stories about Panama travel

www.lasclementinas.com

Manrey Hotel

- Calle Uruguay in the banking district (Calle Uruguay is also the street where most of the night-clubs are located)
- Opened in 2011
- Very hip, modern vibe
- 36 rooms
- Huge, open lobby design is great for one-on-one meetings
- Second level restaurant is considered fine dining and is excellent
- Rooftop restaurant is known for great burgers
- Rooftop poolside bar is one of my favorite places in the city to have a cocktail, watch the sunset and catch some live music (when they have it)
- Really nice rooftop pool
- Both business and vacationers frequent this hotel
- As this hotel is smack in the middle of the night-life scene, it can be loud, especially when staying in rooms that face the street (keep this in mind for Thursday-Sunday stays)

www.manreypanama.com

Hotel El Panama

- In El Cangrejo, on the edge of the banking district
- This is one of the oldest hotels in Panama. Its design is centered around a pool in a huge, open air middle

courtyard. Recent renovations have updated the whole look and feel, but it still has the vibe of a former decade, like an old Howard Johnson but much cooler. I always feel like I've stepped back to the 1950's when I go out into the pool courtyard. I really like this hotel, though I cannot speak to the state of the rooms since they've been updated.

- 344 rooms
- Both vacationers and business people
- Lots of convention business, as the hotel has its own 3,000 seat events center attached to it
- Three restaurants, which serve the typical large hotel fare
- From the low $100s

www.elpanama.com

Country Inn and Suites Amador
(Recently renamed the Country Inn and Suites Panama Canal)

- On the Amador Causeway, next to the Panama Canal
- Some rooms have Canal views
- The Causeway offers great walking/jogging/ biking areas
- 159 mini-suite rooms
- Most popular with budget-minded vacationers
- TGI Friday's restaurant is attached to the hotel – very popular with the locals

- Five minute walk to my favorite expat hangout, the Balboa Yacht Club, for those that want to see the local color
- Large, outdoor pool and lounge area
- Rates from $98

www.countryinns.com/panamacanalpan

Gamboa Rainforest Resort

- Located 30 minutes outside the city on 340 acres within the former Canal Zone in the Soberania National Forest
- 164 rooms
- Gorgeous lobby and restaurant areas overlook the Chagres River
- Full-service Sensory Spa by Clarins
- Wide variety of jungle excursions, eco-tours and adventures
- Popular with tourists
- From the high $100s

www.gamboaresort.com

Holiday Inn Express Financial District

- Located in the banking district on Calle 53
- Opened in 2015
- Modern, clean facilities
- No pool
- Buffet breakfast offered
- Exercise room
- Minimal services offered

77

- Ideal for business or budget-minded travelers
- From the low $100s

www.ihg.com - select Panama hotels

Panama Hilton

- Located on Avenida Balboa, facing Panama Bay
- Five minute walk to the banking district
- Opened in 2014
- Gorgeous restaurants and lobby areas
- 30,000 square feet of events space
- 24-hour small casino
- Full-service spa and fitness center
- Ocean-view Bar Blue on the main level
- Home to Ruth's Chris Steak house
- Service is good, though not fantastic
- Ideal for traveling executives
- From the high $100s

http://www3.hilton.com/en/hotels/panama/hilton-panama-PTYHFHH/index.html

DoubleTree by Hilton Hotel Panama – El Carmen

- Located in Bella Vista
- Walkable to the banking district and many casinos
- Small rooftop pool
- Rooms are loud
- Service practically non-existent by hotel staff (based on my own stay in December 2015)
- Restaurant is mediocre
- Typical budget hotel atmosphere

- Not recommended unless you are young, on a strict budget and don't mind noise
- Specials can run as low as $69

http://doubletree3.hilton.com/en/hotels/panama/doubletree-by-hilton-hotel-panama-city-el-carmen/

American Trade Hotel
- Stunning restored landmark hotel in Casco Viejo (the old city)
- Gorgeous interiors are like stepping into the past
- Ground-floor restaurant atmosphere is good, though the food is only average (and pricey)
- Coffee-shop is cool
- Ideal home base for exploring Casco Viejo on foot
- Some of the best service levels in Panama
- Home to the intimate Danilo's Jazz Club
- Banquet hall can accommodate up to 350 people
- My top choice for a hotel for romance or a luxury stay
- From the mid $300s

https://www.acehotel.com/panama

Note that this list is not exhaustive for all hotels in the city of Panama. There are many, many more. My goal with this list is to give you the local perspective of each of these that I *have* visited, so that you have a local's perspective of what the experience at each might be, other than the promotional material you might see on their websites.

It's also recommended that you check out what's been said by recent guests on TripAdvisor for *any* hotel you may be considering in Panama. Naturally, the rates listed in the list above may change depending on the time of year, or if there's a convention in the hotel the week you are visiting, etc. So, take all of this data with a grain of salt.

(NOTE: You will not find phone numbers as part of this list; however, I do list websites. If those have changed, refer to Google or Trip Advisor. If these names no longer appear there, those particular establishments may have changed names or closed.)

If it were me....

We are frequent travelers, and I always appreciate any insider feedback I can get from those that live in the cities and countries we visit. Here are my thoughts on where to stay from this list, depending on what brings you to Panama.

- If you're young, hip and into partying, stay at the Manrey or the Hard Rock.
- If you're here for business, pick the Le Meridien, the Waldorf Astoria, the Hilton, the Riu or the Marriott.
- If you're here for pleasure and can afford it, stay at Las Clementinas or the American Trade Hotel in Casco Viejo.
- If you're here to meet clients and need to impress them, stay at the Trump, the Hilton, the Waldorf or the American Trade Hotel.
- If you're on a budget and need to be in the city, stay at the El Panama or the Holiday Inn Express.
- If you're here for a conference, stay at the hotel where the conference is being held – it's just easier. That way, you avoid traffic, which can take up a lot of time.

- If you're here looking at Panama as a potential place to live, stay at the El Panama, the Sheraton, or Las Clementinas depending on your budget. These will all give you better access to locals in the restaurants and lobbies for people watching to get a feel for the local color. The Sheraton and El Panama are both centrally located for meeting real estate agents and so forth.

- If you are here for a longer stay (more than a week), I recommend checking out AirBNB.com or FlipKey. com, which offer individually-owned real estate listings for short-term rentals at a variety of levels. I only recommend this if you are going to be here for *more* than a week. Most of these accommodations do not offer room service, so getting your own groceries is necessary. You can access lots of individual reviews on this website as well in addition to the specific listings.

- If you want a beach experience, yet access to the city (20 minutes), stay at the Westin Playa Bonita. The Westin opened in 2012 and in my opinion is the nicer of the two Playa Bonita hotels. You will wish to read the reviews for the Westin carefully however, so that your expectations are realistic related to their service levels.

Taking the Road Less Traveled...

The church in El Valle

Making memories is all about having meaningful experiences, whether you're a visitor or you already live in this beautiful little country. The silver linings we find in our day-to-day experiences is what makes our time on earth memorable and sweet. So, whether you're an expat looking for something new to do, or a tourist visiting the tropics for the first time, you'll want to make note of this resource that will help you experience Panama like a local.

DegustaPanama.com

Foodies, take note, especially if you're just passing through and want something more exciting than the usual tourist traps. Degusta lets you search local eateries by price, popularity, or location, as well as providing a listing of what's new in the market.

Diners create their own user names to rate and comment on restaurants they've frequented. Ratings are averaged in these four categories: food, service, ambience and price. Note that Degusta is currently only provided in Spanish. (Even if you're not a Spanish speaker, you can visit and see how restaurants are rated and make note of phone numbers, addresses, get directions and for some, even make reservations.)

Similar to Yelp or TripAdvisor, Degusta lists how many visitors rated a particular restaurant, shows photos they've posted, and gives specifics on restaurant contact information and hours. It's a wealth of information for finding a meal that fits your budget and your taste.

Travel Tip for flying to the San Blas Islands
When the national airline enforced the 15 lb. weight limit for my luggage to get to a remote location on one of our trips, I used a contact lens case to hold my liquid facial soap and moisturizer. Each side held enough for a three-day supply, and I could leave the 3-ounce bottles behind.

6

Doing Business in Panama

Mobile vendors selling water on the highway

THE REPUBLIC OF Panama has risen significantly in the world's eye in recent years, which is very likely the reason you picked up this book. Nowhere is this more true than in the business opportunities that have exploded in the region.

Business is booming here alongside the $5.2 billion expansion of the Panama Canal, which is scheduled to be completed late this year in 2016. In 2015, 2.5 million tourists visited Panama according to an article in Panama's daily newspaper *La Prensa* on 12/31/15. In past years, more than 60% of those visitors came for business purposes. The capital's skyline boasts spectacular architecture on the Pacific Bay as evidence of the last decade's real estate boom. The national government is offering significant pro-business benefits specific to certain areas and/or industries. Many companies have taken notice.

With its expanding profile, forward-thinking businesses have come to Panama in hopes of capturing a piece of its tropical treasure on their balance sheets. Unfortunately, many of them are not fully clear that the ways of conducting business in Panama are very different from anywhere else. What appears at first glance to function as 'business as usual' is a far cry from what most professionals have experienced elsewhere.

Day-to-day Business Realities

In the first book in this series, you can read about cultural differences in efficiency and business attire. But what else is different? I worked as a business executive for eight years in the city of Panama. Here are some observations from that experience.

Business Hours

Most business offices open for the day at 9 a.m. and close between 5 and 6 p.m. Monday through Friday, with the exception of banks. Banks normally open at 9 a.m. and close between 3:30 and 5 p.m., depending on location. Retail shops close between 5 and 9 p.m.

Note that these are the norms in the city of Panama. In the interior, opening hours vary according to local demand.

Keeping Appointments

It's common in Panama to confirm an appointment on the day the appointment is scheduled to take place. Don't be surprised if you receive a phone, text or email confirming an appointment that is supposed to happen only an hour later. People here are terrified that you will forget them, or that you won't show up, so they take this precaution, as a balance against not getting stood up. It will seem strange at first, but get used to it. Once you've been stood up a dozen times, you'll probably take the practice up yourself!

Canceling an appointment at the exact time the meeting was supposed to start is also very common here. I can't count the number of calls I received that said, "Oh, I'm so sorry, but Mr. Jose can't make the meeting today." Usually, this is anywhere from five to 20 minutes past the hour the meeting was supposed to start! Don't sweat it. It's not personal.

Meetings

Panamanians love to have meetings. They prefer to meet you in person rather then to conduct business over the phone or via email. This is due to three things.

First, participating in a meeting makes everyone feel important because they get to express their ideas at length. In the Panama business culture, decisions are often reached only *after* everyone has had their chance to express an opinion and contribute to the discussion. (This can be very eye opening and frustrating for Gringos who are used to making a decision based on efficiency and data alone.)

Meetings in Panama can last from one to four hours. No matter what, expect that the discussion that you might *think* (with your Gringo tendencies) could have been done and accomplished via email will take at least an hour here in an in-person meeting, and most likely, longer.

Second, meetings provide an opportunity to build trust between the involved parties. Building trust is vital to getting business done in Panama. Often, three or four meetings are required before an agreement is ever made, solely for this reason.

Third, meetings are more the norm in Panama because there's been a lot of corruption in the past in this culture. Having a face-to-face meeting requires the parties involved to be there in person, and that means there's less possibility of something being falsified or out of place. This is especially true in banking. People here like to look you in the eye, face-to-face. That's not a bad thing.

Another reason that meetings take so long is because they rarely start on time. The accepted norm is that parties will arrive 15-20 minutes after the agreed-upon hour, and then between the niceties of asking about family, and talk of social things, and being served coffee, it's another ten minutes before any business topic is broached. All of these are social norms. So, check your impatience at the door, and relax.

Take into account that if someone else comes into the meeting after everyone else has already been seated, the meeting will be further delayed with the additional introduction and the incoming party greeting everyone else in the room one-by-one.

Lunch Breaks

People in Panama are religious about their lunch breaks. If there's a set hour for an employee lunch break, the sign will go up in front of your nose and they will depart, even if you have been standing in their line for an hour. It does not matter. The lunch hour is strictly observed, and customer service is normally not taken into consideration.

In an office setting, similarly, your Panamanian counterparts and employees will take their full hour *to the minute* to sit and eat their lunch, no matter what. It's rarely culturally acceptable for you to expect that someone work through their lunch hour unless it's an absolute emergency. Nope. It does not matter if the boss wants that report done ASAP, it can wait. And it will wait. The lunch hour is required by law, just like it is in other countries, but in Panama, the employee *knows this right* and they will take every minute they are owed. It's part of the working class mindset in the country.

Establishing Credibility

Most companies new to Panama don't fully comprehend the value of establishing credibility in the local marketplace. Nor do they understand how to do it according to Panamanian business culture. They simply have not discovered the rules of the local game. But, alas, there's no written rulebook that's handed out at the local Chamber of Commerce. In fact, that's part of the game – you have to figure out the road map for yourself, and it's not easy terrain to follow.

Following are five steps to establishing professional credibility in the Panamanian market.

First, relocate one of your executives to the country to live full-time. Countless companies believe they can send an executive down for a week or two a month, and establish business here. Bottom line, it does not work. Panamanians want to know you've made a real commitment to the country. Being here means you're serious, so you have to actually be here to be taken seriously.

Second, physically lease or purchase an office space in the city or the market close to your potential clients. Appearance is everything in business culture, so when you select your location, make sure it's a top-notch place where you'd be proud to host executives from your client firms.

Third, hire some locals as soon as you can. Perhaps this seems like a no-brainer, but surprisingly, it's not. Panamanians are keen to know you're contributing to the strength of the local economy with your pocketbook. Local search firms can help to identify the right talent for your firm.

Fourth, get personally involved in local business associations. Attend networking events weekly to meet your clients, competitors and vendors. Take them to lunch and dinner as a way of getting to know them better as people. Relationships in Latin culture drive business. You may buy eight meals over a year before your client actually signs a contract with you. This is normal. Building trust takes time.

Fifth, have patience. Like the popular Finesse shampoo commercial from the 1970's said, "Shampoo. Rinse. Repeat."

The same concept is true for business in Panama. Building a reputation locally takes a *significant* amount of time and patience. Getting your name known and your brand established does not happen overnight, nor does it happen with the speed that many companies experience in other markets. Commit to a two- to three-year timeline for company solvency in this market. Expecting anything else is unreasonable, and will lead to frustration and dissatisfaction.

The things you don't know about the local business culture are the ones that will sink you. The five tips above, if followed in order and with sincerity, will lead to a company's long-term success in the local market. Those that make the commitment will reap the rewards from the opportunities that abound in the Panama market.

Need more help?

If your company needs more help and direction, get in touch with me. I know a number of consultants who may be able to assist you in your local set-up.

7

FINDING THE RIGHT (PRIVATE) SCHOOL

Native children in an Embera Indian village

THE NUMBER ONE concern most expats have when they move to Panama is finding quality education for their children. Happily, there are many more options now than there were several years ago. The bottom line for all expats is that they will want to put their children in private school. The country's public school system is very poorly ranked, and is not normally a consideration for expat families moving to Panama.

Private schools do have a cost, of course, and that should be accounted for in your plans, as you consider the cost of living in Panama for you and your family. Many expats that move to Panama are fortunate to have what's called an expat package, which their company provides to them for living and schooling expenses as part of their cost of living benefits. (Transferring expats, if you have not been offered an expat package as part of your benefits and are in the midst of negotiating, you'll want to ensure you get that into the mix.)

Private school tuition in Panama can cost anywhere from $300 to $2000 per month per child. There's also a fee called a Capital Investment fee that is normally charged per child by the private school when your child enrolls for the first time. This can be as high as $10,000 to $15,000. This is normally a non-refundable fee. Some schools provide a lump sum discount on the capital investment fee if several siblings are enrolling simultaneously; be sure to ask.

I highly recommend that when you visit Panama, you visit the schools you are considering for one-on-one interviews with the administrators and teachers. Tour each campus and visit the individual facilities. Every one of them offers something slightly different. Do not assume that just because a school teaches English that it is the right place for your child. This decision is vital to the health of your family as you acclimate and find your way in this country.

Schools in the city

Here's an alphabetical list of some of the top private schools in Panama. All of these are English speaking with classes taught in English, unless otherwise noted. Spanish is also taught in each, in addition to other languages.

Balboa Academy
www.balboaacademy.org

Boston School
www.bostonschool.com.pa

International School of Panama (ISP)
www.isp.edu.pa

King's College
www.kingscollege.com.pa

Knightsbridge Schools International Panama (KSIP)
www.ksi-panama.com

Lycee Francais Paul Gaugin de Panama
www.lfpanama.com
   Classes taught primarily in French, with both English and Spanish as second languages

Metropolitan School
www.themetropolitanschool.com

Verify the level of accreditation and curriculum each school provides, to be sure it offers what your child needs now and for the future. This is especially important if your long-term plans for your child include a return to the U.S. or other more developed nation.

Panama has attracted a number of new international-level schools in the past few years. The increasing number of expats moving to Panama in recent years has created a demand for more and better schooling for their children. The availability of quality schools continues to add to the country's attraction for many expats and families considering moving to Panama. It's likely that this trend will continue.

Schools in the Interior (west of the city)

Certainly, private school offerings are available to expats outside the metropolis of Panama. However, they are few and far between. I'm aware of two private schools in Boquete and two in the Coronado area on the Pacific side, though there may be more sprouting up. Other than speaking to other expats who live in these areas, it's recommended you ask for details about these options from your real estate broker.

Check with your Embassy

The local embassy for your home country in Panama may also be a good resource for obtaining a listing of international-level schools that cater to their citizens. Since each country's educational system varies from one place to the next, any additional insight from an official source like this could be to your advantage while you are on your fact-finding mission.

For future expats from the U.S. and Canada, a call to your local Foreign Service office in your closest major metropolitan city may garner you the same information.

8
Tropical Adjustments

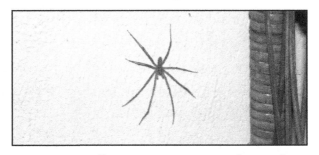

A visitor on my wall one morning measured six inches across

Creepy Crawly Realities

Most of us have grown up with a proclivity for steering clear of things that go bump in the night. The same is usually true for the desire to interact closely with most bugs, spiders, snakes and the things that crawl on any number of legs, especially when it comes to these creatures invading your personal space.

In tropical environments, these critters abound in all shapes, forms and sizes. Here's a few thoughts on making your interactions with them as limited as possible.

Rock and roll

Critters like to hide, behind and under stationary things, especially if the items have been in one place for a period of time. When you need to move something that's been on the floor or in a stationary position for a while, first give it a tap with your foot. If the item is heavy, rock it gently so that it moves slightly. Then, use your toe (with shoes on) to slowly roll the item over. Scorpions have a tendency to attach themselves to the bottom of things, so this will give you a clear visual of what's underneath before you proceed to move anything with bare hands.

The combined rock and roll motion gives any creepy occupant the heads up to get a move on, so there'll be less chance of an unpleasant encounter.

Tread heavily

You've probably heard the advice – tread lightly – in the past, but that's the last thing you want to do when hiking in areas where there's lots of dense trees, vines and fallen leaves.

Tom O'Keefe, an eight-year Panama resident and an avid outdoorsman, shares this advice, "If you're a hiker, always wear long pants and boots. Watch where you're hiking. Don't go in areas that are clearly marked "Do Not Enter," as those signs are there for a reason. Otherwise, it's a good idea to walk with a firm step. When you do this, any animal residents or snakes will feel the vibrations and generally, get out of your way."

Shake, shake, shake

Bugs, lizards, geckos, spiders, scorpions and snakes like to nest and hang out in cooler areas. Before you get into bed at night, turn on the light and give every layer of your bedding a complete fluff. This gives you a visual confirmation that you won't have any multi-legged creatures waiting for you, as you get tucked in.

A call to Alexandra, the Panamanian vet tech who took care of our dog for many years, yielded a similar recommendation for pets. "Many pets will have an allergic reaction to an insect or spider bite, just like a human would. But with pets, those reactions can cause death." Apparently, pets can suffer as much as (or more than) humans do from an unplanned encounter with a poisonous critter, due to their lower body weight.

"Often an allergic reaction from a spider bite or a scorpion sting can cause suffocation, and even death," she told me. Pets are more prone to seek out cooler environments in tropical heat, which can lead to an increased chance of critter interactions.

Run the tap

In many tropical rentals and weekend homes that don't get daily use, geckos, centipedes, and scorpions will crawl up the drains into bathtubs, showers and sinks. When you arrive or check in, turn on the tap in every bathroom or maid's room, and let the water run for 3-5 minutes. This will flush the intruders down or out right away. Otherwise, you might discover them when you're naked and shoeless, which won't necessarily be the kind of relaxation you were hoping to find. This is especially common during the dry (or summer) season in Panama, which is early to mid December through April.

Keep your boots on

In some tropical locations, it's best to keep your shoes on at all times, unless you're physically on the beach in the sand. Stepping on a scorpion in some parts of Latin America can lead to a dangerous allergic reaction or even death. In Panama, scorpions are more frequent between December and April, especially in the Interior areas along the Pacific beaches, which have slightly drier climates. When in these areas during these months, it's recommended to keep your shoes on, even while inside, to avoid any painful foot encounters.

Take a look at these descriptions of tropical critters, common to Panama.

Geckos

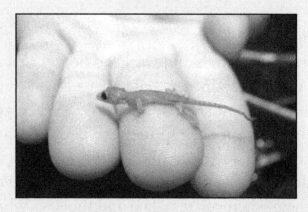

In many cultures, the presence of the gecko is believed to constitute good luck for your household. In Panama, that's not a common belief, but you will certainly find these little guys everywhere. The gecko is not a dangerous creature. In Panama, these are usually transparent to yellow-color lizards, with amphibious, frog-like skin and features. They eat mosquitos and insects, and make a noise referred to as "chuffing".

Even if you're not a person who enjoys creepy crawlies, you do get used to these guys being around. In fact, they become so familiar that you might even find yourself having conversations with them when you see them in the same places over and over again. We got so accustomed to them that we began to consider them members of the family. ☺ They are especially handy because they help keep the mosquito population down.

Geckos are common in every tropical environment in Central and South America.

Butterflies

Butterflies abound in Panama everywhere you look. In fact, the name 'Panama' actually means 'abundance of butterflies' according to local belief because so many species exist here. I became a fan of carrying my iPhone with me at all times, whether walking the dog or shelling on the beach, because I invariably encountered a new kind of butterfly that I'd never seen before when I was least expecting it.

In truth, most butterflies you'll find in Panama actually fall into the moth family, but that does not make them any less spectacular. Blue, green, yellow, red, orange, and with every design you can imagine – they are here, or they're flying through at some point. And, they come in all sizes. Get your camera ready, because these little (and big) guys are quite spectacular.

The Smithsonian Tropical Research Institute is based in Panama. It's always educational to refer to their online library to locate a moth or butterfly that you've discovered on your Panama journey. (http://www.sil.si.edu/imagegalaxy/imageGalaxy_collResult.cfm?term=Butterflies%20and%20Moths)

Scorpions

The scorpion has the same body style as a lobster with a hard shell, eight legs, two pinchers, and a curved tail ending in a pointed stinger. These scary-looking guys measure one to six inches long in the tropics, in colors of translucent white, tan, dark brown, brick red, or black. Scorpions come in both venomous and non-venomous varieties, and their stings are extremely painful. Happily, in Panama, the venomous variety is less than 2% of the local population, but it's better to be safe than sorry if you get stung with a quick trip to the clinic to get treated. (Refer to chapter 4 for the story of my own scorpion sting.)

Spiders (in general)

There are too many varieties of spiders to list, as they abound in every tropical country in the world. Some are indigenous to drier climates: others to humidity, but they all have one thing in common: they're everywhere. You'll find them in the forest, at the beach, in your apartment, in dark places, in closets, in their webs, on the ground, and just about anywhere else.

In Panama, common species are jumping spiders and wandering spiders, though you'll also find tarantulas, brown recluses, and hundreds of other types. Spiders are an important part of the global food chain, so it's best to relocate them versus killing them, if you can encourage them to get out of your personal space.

Jumping Spiders

These little guys are very small, usually ¼–½ inch long. They have furry, fuzzy hair, large eyes and thick legs. They can jump up to a foot at a time, in any direction. Coloration varies from blonde to brown to black.

Snakes

Reportedly, around 130 species of snakes exist in the Republic of Panama. These vary in color, size and shape, and both venomous and non-venomous comprise part of that count. Most encounters might occur when the weather is cooler, or you are traveling through a tropical forest where the weather is cooler due to tree cover. Reportedly, most snake bites happen when the snake gets stepped on. Most poisonous snakes in Panama are pretty small, measuring between six and twelve inches.

Most of the time, snakes will do their best to get out of the area when they hear you approaching. If you encounter one, keep your distance in order to avoid any chance of a bite. If you do get bit, physicians prefer that you either bring the snake with you or a piece of the snake with you so that it can be identified. This will help determine if a dose of anti-venom is in order to counteract the bite. (Note: It's probably best to kill the snake before you take it with you, if you get bit.)

In our first year in Panama, a 9-foot boa constrictor was found behind our condominium building by the gardener. The environmental protection agency was called, and it took three men to carry this beauty to a truck to be transported to safer territory. (Boa constrictors are a protected species.)

There's a small, rustic *Serpenteria* (live snake exhibit and refuge) in El Valle, Panama. The curator there is usually the one that's called to identify a snake when someone has been bit (anywhere in the country). If you're in the area, it's worth a visit to see the different species, especially the poisonous ones.

Tropical Temps: What you need to know about Panama's weather

Depending on where you come from, you may be accustomed to a climate that delivers four seasons each and every year.

In Panama, you'll only have two. Since Panama sits just 500 miles north of the equator, the two local seasons are easily defined: hot and hotter. This is the tropics, after all! Formally, they're known as the Dry season (or Summer) and the Rainy (or Green) season.

The local populations usually tell you they enjoy the dry season the best. We grew to appreciate the rainy season over time, mostly because during those months, it's slightly cooler and the beaches are less crowded.

Palmar Beach on the Pacific side

Summer: The Dry Season

The dry season, locally referred to as Summer, begins in mid December and goes through the end of April. In recent years, it has stretched to the end of May. (Some reference global warming as the cause of that.)

Characteristics of the dry season are temperatures in the low to mid 90s Farenheit, with occasional days soaring upwards to 100. Keep in mind that the city of Panama will be hotter than areas like Boquete or El Valle, which have (slightly) higher elevations. Other areas like David and the Azuero Peninsula can get even hotter. A number of microclimates within Panama also exist.

The school year for most educational institutions in Panama (with the exception of the international ones) runs from late February through mid December. The two-month break for summer vacation for most of the country's children coincides with the dry season. What that means for you is that you'll see most families taking time off from work between January and April (sometimes up to a month at a time), and traveling within the Isthmus.

In the dry season, traffic will be heavier, and hotel rates will increase. Beaches will be more crowded, especially on weekends. When you're in the city, you'll notice more tourists, and a steady flow of cruise ships docking overnight in the Bay. The number of visitors increases significantly in the entire country in Summer, especially in hotels, casinos, restaurants, the historic districts like Casco Viejo and Panama Viejo, and in the malls.

During Summer, very little rain falls, if any. The skies are a spectacular blue every day, often punctuated with puffy white clouds. Even though you are in a tropical environment, you'll notice that the country's lush landscape will dry up, slightly, and turn lighter shades of green and brown.

Panama does have deciduous trees, and some of these will drop their leaves during the summer months, which may remind you of fall and winter in many North America states.

It's a common misconception that a tropical climate means that only palm trees grow in Panama. In fact, because we have tropical rainforest, more types of trees grow in Panama than in most other places in the world. There's a reason that the Smithsonian Research Institute has a number of research stations in the country.

Another cultural experience:
Driving to the beach in the summer

Because summer means more tourists, and more locals taking vacation time, the traffic within the country increases substantially. This is especially the case in the city and getting to and from the Pacific Coast beaches. Culturally, locals and expats alike head for the beach on the weekends. That driving experience from the city to the beach and back again on Friday afternoons, Saturdays and Sundays is chaotic, crazy and sometimes even dangerous.

In 2012, Panama's English newspaper – *The Visitor* – published a short advice column I wrote (as a ghost columnist) about this driving experience. Until you partake of this particular adventure yourself, it's hard to fully get the picture. This piece attempts to capture the humor of what this sojourn was like from my perspective on many, many back-and-forth trips from the city to the Pacific side.

Jill's Roadway Rules (for the Summer)

It's summertime again in Panama! The mercury's rising higher. Kids are on vacation. City traffic is a bit easier, because Moms are sleeping in. And weekends? Everybody heads for the beach.

If you've lived in Panama for any amount of time, you've probably got a few tales to tell about your own experiences of driving on the *Panamericana*. Am I right? Maybe you're new to town, and have yet to venture toward the Interior. Either way, good news! I've outlined a few road rules below that – if followed – will bring some sanity to your beach driving experience.

Now, these may sound like they're only for your neighbor, but don't judge before you read. It's usually those that think they own the road that need the most reminders, in my experience. So, listen up.

- Chatty Cathy, hang up the phone. Does your friend that's just ten minutes behind you really need to know exactly where you are? And don't even make me mention texting, please. Just put down the phone and drive.

- Mario Andretti, stay left. And by that, I mean all the way left. Especially where the lane markings are undefined on the Autopista through Chorrera. There's no reason to pass on the right, even when you can get away with it. It's rude and unnecessary. No *Juega Vivo*!

- Slowpoke, you know who you are. Keep your car right. You're welcome to drive as slow as you like, but the view from the right side of the road is where you really should be if you're going to have to check out every little thing that happens on the drive. (Plus, it will help keep brother Andretti where he should be.)

- Speedy Gonzalez, when construction zones narrow down to a lane or two, and the traffic gets backed up, please just stay in your lane. Zooming around a total of four cars is not really going to get you there any faster. Plus, by the time you try to force your way in on me, you'll find I'm not going to be very accommodating, no matter how many times you honk.

Safety (and sanity) on the road starts with you and me. If we expect others to behave on the road, let's set the example. Perhaps it'd make the beach drive less like a video game and more like a cruise. The reason to go to the beach is to relax, right? So, what if we took that concept to the road? Hmm…food for thought. Happy summer, everyone!

For more on driving in Panama, and how you'll need to adjust, refer to the first book in the Gringo Guide to Panama series. It's a must read for first-timers and any tourist thinking they want to rent a car on their first trip to the country. (By the way, said behavior is highly discouraged, if you want to live through your first visit and leave with any sanity.)

The Change of the Seasons

Tropical rainforest

As mentioned previously, Summer slides into the Green season around the end of April. That means Easter has come and gone. In North America, the coming month of May brings Mother's Day and flower buds and the height of Spring.

For most of us from the North, Spring means new beginnings, a shaking off of Winter, and a fresh start to being outdoors. For me personally, I used to love annual Spring Cleaning, when I'd give my house a thorough cleaning out, which was refreshing both spatially and emotionally.

Now, here you are in Panama. Perhaps your mental calendar says that Spring is beginning (or in full swing), but in the tropics, you've now entered the period where the heat of Summer begins to dissolve into the Rainy/Green season. Your body clock may feel a bit confused. This is the case for many expats, especially in their first year living in the country.

In Panama, Easter's passing means there's only one holiday left on the local holiday schedule as Summer concludes (May 1, Labor Day). Because many Gringos are so accustomed to the U.S. holidays beginning in May, this lack of days off in the middle of the year can feel a little strange.

Holiday / Seasonal Adjustments

In the U.S., April's advent means Spring is heading quickly into Summer, including the celebration of three big American holidays: Memorial Day, Fourth of July and Labor Day.

In Panama after May 1, the national calendar doesn't grace us with another local holiday until early November

(*Días Patrias*). This can be a pretty big adjustment for those of us with seasonal time clocks accustomed to barbeques and fireworks from May to September. (For more on this topic, refer to Chapter 10.)

At first, you may not think much of it. But then those holidays arrive, and you see old friends from back home on Facebook and Twitter celebrating. The nostalgia hits you when you're least expecting it. You might be sitting in the office with a cup of Joe, doing your daily grind. You send an email to one of your Northern counterparts and an auto-reply kicks back with the cruel reminder that they're off and you're not. That's when you really miss it.

Welcome to the seasonal blues. It happens to every expat at some point in time. For you, seasonal blues may exhibit as illness, mild depression, or may blossom into an intense longing to be closer to friends and family. Some of us get the urge to hop a flight just to be back at that picnic table for the Fourth of July with loved ones, baked beans and potato salad. All of this is *completely* normal, especially during your first two years living abroad.

Help for Homesickness

So, what to do? First, know that the pain of change is temporary. The discomfort of unfamiliar cultural experiences lessens with time. Through the years, you'll begin to understand and enjoy local customs. You may even adopt Panama's traditions and make them your own. But at first, it's safe to assume you'll have your transition period, just as one season slides into another.

To alleviate homesickness, seek out places where you can meet and hang with other expats. Being with others who have sailed the same waters that you are traversing can help. One popular expat gathering spot is the Balboa Yacht Club in Amador. Many others can be found in the ads and listings of the local English newspaper, *The Visitor*.

Other mechanisms to help you cope are the same things you would do anywhere else: get regular exercise, connect to a church or community group, or take up a new hobby.

Finally, make technology your best friend. With Skype, WhatsApp and other free communication platforms available online, it's easier than ever to stay connected with those back home.

Sometimes transition is easy and sometimes it's not. If you give yourself the permission to experience your feelings, and figure out what makes you feel better in the interim, you'll make it through just fine.

Winter: The Rainy (or Green) Season

The rain has begun. Daytime temperatures have fallen from the 90s to a more amenable low to mid 80s. Once the sun goes down, you can look forward to temps in the mid 70s, most of the time. The humidity is higher, because it's likely raining every day at some point. But the rain in Panama even during the rainy season is not constant, like in Seattle or Paris. Instead, in some months, the rain comes and goes. In other months, it comes and stays – with force – for hours at a time. But, then it stops, and the sun comes out again, or a milky overcast sky emerges, and the humidity envelopes you like a glove.

At times, you will feel like you can hardly breathe, because the humidity is so thick.

Welcome to the rainy season, or the 'green' season, as the country's tourism board coined the wetter months of the Panama's year in 2009. And 'tis the season of green. The rainy season begins after an (estimated) three months of transition from Summer in May through July with a little rain happening here and there. Then from July to early September, the rain continues every day for about an hour or so, but not all day, and you'll still see a lot of sun. The big difference is that the humidity climbs. (Think 90-98% humidity during this time. You really feel it because your clothes stick to you when you walk out the front door, even right after you've had a shower.)

Don't worry. You do get used to it. Plus, the nights are a little bit cooler.

Then one day, in late September or early October, the height of the rainy season starts. While it's hard to pinpoint an exact date when it happens, when it does, you will know. Suddenly, one afternoon, the heavy rain starts and then it comes every single day for hours at a time.

During the height of the rainy season in October and November, you'll wake to overcast skies, with occasional sun, and that will become your norm. Some nights it will rain all night. And on others, it won't rain at all. During these two months, the humidity increases to its highest possible point of the year. You'll notice a significant difference, believe me. Skies stay a consistent gray or milky white, and the highest percentage of rainfall occurs.

Indian Summer

Breakthrough days of all sun and no rain will happen from time to time within the seven months of the Green season, with two periods being commonly known as Indian Summer. Historically, these fall in a two-week period at the end of June, and another two-week period in mid to late September. There's no guarantee of this, but a break from the rain and brilliant blue skies do seem to emerge every year in these two periods with regularity. And, when they do, everyone breathes a sigh of relief and is reminded of just how spectacular Summer can be.

How Panama's rain differs

When it starts raining in Panama, it *really* rains. I equate it to God turning on a faucet, because that's what it feels like. The skies open up and the water falls straight down with such force that it uproots trees, floods roads in minutes, and sweeps people off their feet. Accompanying strong winds and spectacular light shows with heavy thunder make Panama's rains something to see.

At other times, the rain is soft and steady, but still falls straight down. When you live here, you'll get used to always having an umbrella with you – in your purse, in your car, by your front door, in your office. Because if you don't, you won't just get wet when you get caught in the rain, you'll get *drenched*.

In my first year of working in Panama, I would often get frustrated with some of the members of my work team at the office who would get caught by a storm and not return to the office within the standard lunch hour. The reason? They'd neglected to take an umbrella with them. So, when a storm hit, they would stand under cover (or stay in their cars) until the rain abated, which could be from 20 minutes up to an hour or more beyond their lunch hour. My thinking was typical of a Gringo mindset: *Why did they not plan ahead and take an umbrella? It's rainy season, for God's sake!*

How much rain does Panama receive each year? On the Pacific side, rainfall totals an average of 80 inches per year. On the Caribbean side, it totals an average of 120 inches per year. Compare that to annual rainfall from wherever you've moved from, to really appreciate how much that is.

In the month of November, the country receives more rain than in any other month of the year. It's rare for the rain to fall all day, every day. Sometimes, a storm will start in the late evening and will go all night. When this happens – maybe 8-10 nights a year – I find this time period incredibly refreshing and relaxing.

Surprisingly, many locals tell me they don't like it. You'll notice your coworkers and neighbors emerging from their homes in jackets and sweaters when it rains, especially for several days in a row.

I found this amusing at first, because it's still normally in the low 80s Farenheit in the daytime, and to me, that feels warm. But with time, I understood that Panamanians consider October and November the height of their winter. (For expats from regions where snow actually falls, rain and 80s temperatures are hardly categorized as winter.)

Because there's so much moisture, the resulting temperatures can almost feel cold, when you have lived in Panama for some time. The culmination of all the rain results in spectacular vivid landscapes, come early January. The end of the rainy season is when the country is at its most lush and its most green. (Planning Tip: For you photographers, this is the time when Panama is at its most photogenic.)

Insider Tip: If you live in the city of Panama, you may wish to elect to buy a car or SUV that has a higher carriage than a normal sedan, due to the flash floods that can occur in a few hours in certain areas of the city after significant rainfall. Otherwise, you'll find that roads in some areas are simply impassable – especially when it's high tide – as the rainwater has nowhere to recede to, and the water levels bring everything to a screeching halt.

How the Green season feels

(A personal reverie one October evening)

I sigh with contentment, as I sink into my favorite lawn chair on our covered patio. The gauge reads a mild 79 degrees, but to me, it feels like heaven. These are the nights I don my lightest pair of cotton pants and an oversized t-shirt from my husband's closet. I pretend I'm back Stateside in the Midwest U.S., and for a few minutes at least, I see myself back there, where autumn is turning to winter. For a moment, it sounds like it too, with Sunday night NFL football streaming on the laptop.

A friend attended a conference in my hometown last week. There, the leaves are falling in hues of red and gold. The air is crisp and dry, requiring a warm sweater and tall boots. Scary décor adorns front porches, awaiting Halloween trick-or-treaters. The days are getting shorter, hurrying families home to warm fireplaces and hearty soups. The rise and fall of the seasons is one of my favorite things. Though I enjoy Panama, I miss the seasons.

When you've come from cooler climates, the adjustment to year-round tropical temps can feel strange. It can take years to get used to the regularity of our 12-hour sunrise to sundown daily schedule. While I cherish the beauty of a deep tan and naked manicured feet the whole year through, I also recall with fondness the smooth feel of leather jackets. Suede boots. Angora turtlenecks. Cozy scarves and fitted gloves.

When you yearn for a respite even cooler than the lovely nights October brings to Panama, I recommend an escape to fresher climates like El Valle or Boquete in Panama's Interior, or a short flight over to Bogota or Medellin, Colombia.

Meanwhile, breathe deeply and cherish the coolest temps you'll have all year in Panama. It's not Autumn, but take comfort in the dry cleaning costs you're saving by wearing swimsuits and shorts. And don't forget to savor those spectacular shades of green, everywhere you look.

When is the best time to visit Panama?

The answer to this question really depends on why you are visiting the country. If you're only coming for tourism, then I recommend the dry season. If you're coming to live, then I recommend you come at least once during each season before you move, so that you have a chance to experience a little bit of each.

9
MAKING MERRY AT THE HOLIDAYS

*The old public bus system – called Diablos Rojos (Red Devils)
are adorned in colorful graffiti*

ONE OF THE things I noticed in the first year we lived in Panama was that most of us as human beings get pretty used to the way we've always done things: in our culture, in our families, and in the rhythms of our lives. Something as big as a transatlantic move to another country turns all of those rhythms upside down, and uncovers just how attached we've become over the years to those cultural norms. As you've read in the prior chapters, the rhythms of your new life in Panama will be very different from those you experienced wherever you used to live.

The Holiday Calendar

Nowhere is this more evident than in Panama's holiday calendar. If you've hailed from North America, and especially from the United States, your annual holidays fall for the most part between Memorial Day (in late May) to Labor Day (in early September), which constitutes the bulk of the U.S. summertime period.

In Panama, the entire holiday schedule is celebrated between November 1 and May 1, with the bulk of the holidays falling within November, December and February.

In the first year, with all the other adjustments we were making in our new life in Panama, the holiday calendar differences were hardly noticeable to me. The dates of the Panamanian holidays that took place in February, April and May felt a little strange, but I looked at them as added bonuses. Because I had just transferred from working in the U.S., my system was still in sync with the holiday schedule there.

The end of Panama's holiday schedule concludes in early May with the celebration of the country's Labor Day.

In the U.S., on the other hand, the summer holiday schedule is just getting started with Memorial Day weekend. It wasn't until I was working in my office in Panama on the Thursday before Memorial Day in 2008, that I felt like I was missing something.

Think of how many Memorial Day barbeques you've been a part of over the years. How about July 4th family reunions? And family get-aways for Labor Day before school started?

It was as I approached each of these holidays (that were no longer holidays in my working calendar in Panama) that I realized the significance each of them had had in our lives emotionally and as rituals of our home culture.

The absence of these holiday get-togethers with family and friends kicked off a serious bout of homesickness for me that first year. As I reflected on what holiday times had meant to us as markers of our lives over the years, I began to appreciate even more the rhythm and comfort and significance those dates bring in our culture.

It's funny how we don't necessarily appreciate those things until we no longer have them, isn't it? Ah yes, I had discovered yet one more thing to appreciate about being an expat.

Many new expats find that adjusting to a new holiday schedule in Panama is a big cultural adjustment. Others, less so. Whatever this turns out looking like for you, over the years, you'll likely come to adopt Panama's holiday schedule with gusto, and make them your own.

Let me share some of the other idiosyncracies that make Panama's holidays observances unique in the following paragraphs.

Some Dates: A Moving Target

Here's a funny idiosyncracy about Panama that is pretty unusual: Panama has holiday dates that are often moved by the government, as needed.

I'd never personally experienced this to the level that we've seen it happen here in Panama. Certainly, in the U.S., holiday celebrations are not moved for July 4th or Christmas. I don't recall the U.S. President declaring a certain holiday be moved, in order for it to fall on another date than the one on which it is normally celebrated.

Here in Panama, this practice is somewhat the norm. At least twice a year, when the government realizes that a certain holiday falls on a weekend day instead of during the week, they will change it.

Take the Independence from Spain holiday as it fell in 2012 as an example. The date for this holiday is November 28th. (That's the date in history the country's independence from Spain was declared.) In 2012, the 28th fell on a Wednesday. Ten days before, on November 18, the President declared that the holiday would be moved to Monday, November 26th. (Note: He didn't just say it would be *observed* on Monday: he officially *moved* the date.) Of course, all my employees were thrilled: another three-day weekend!

This practice happens with regularity here – most often when the official in power is struggling in popularity for some reason or another – and the moving of the holiday seems to buoy or increase their ratings at least for a period of time.

This movement of holidays example of why *flexibility* is a key component of your success when you move to Panama: because you never know what might just be around the corner.

Because if you planned meetings for the day (like November 26) or happened to have had personal appointments scheduled – like to get a haircut or have your teeth cleaned – you might as well cancel them, because they will not be happening. (And, you can't expect that the place where you had the appointments would think to call you and reschedule, until the day *after* the holiday has taken place.)

Hopefully, because you've already read the first Gringo Guide to Panama and you're already this far through this book, you'd probably already thought of that. Am I right?

Halloween: Where did all the ghouls go?

Reportedly, Halloween is now the most-celebrated holiday in the U.S. Hmmmm. I find that interesting, because that certainly wasn't the case when we left the States in 2008.

Yes, it was celebrated. By both adults and kids alike. But I've always been of the opinion that Halloween was more for kids. (Though I do recall multiple costume parties where we participated with major celebration with all of our adult friends.)

Halloween was always a big deal for us growing up in the U.S. and especially for our children, with activities in the suburb we lived in. The kids always had annual parties at their schools. Area malls hosted safe trick or treating nights. For college kids, it was a cultural phenomenon to party on campus or in area bars and restaurants.

So, what about Halloween in Panama?

One of the big challenges of raising kids in Panama is that you're always looking for things to do. Halloween is no exception. Events and activities related to Halloween in

Panama seem to be more focused in small circles versus widespread.

For school-aged children, you'll find that Halloween is mostly limited to at-school activities, with a few home parties hosted by one of your children's friends. Invitees are usually specific to the grade of the party-thrower. For teenagers, it's the same thing. This year, I didn't even hear about a children's dress-up party. In the States, there'd be at least 50 invitations, and some that would have to be turned down!

For the crowd that's of age (and in Panama, the drinking age is 18), a few bars usually advertise a costumed night out. But, again, this year there was one lonely ad visible in the English speaking newspaper. One tour company did a Canal cruise and a costume was required to get on board. But, that was about the extent of it.

Strange, isn't it? For a country so enamored with Carnival (better know as *Mardi Gras* to you U.S. readers) and all the hoopla that goes with it, you might think there'd be wider celebration for something like Halloween. But that's simply not the case.

According to my Panamanian colleagues, in 2012, a number of local churches began a fierce campaign to ban Halloween as a celebration in Panama. Panama is 85% Catholic, and the church holds major sway. There's no doubt that these efforts have had some significant impact in the lack of local celebrations.

For those of you that have children, it's probably best to create your own Halloween customs – something the little ones can do at school or with their friends. Otherwise, you might as well save the pumpkins from becoming Jack-o-Lanterns and instead use them in a pie come November.

November: Celebrating Independence

Whereas many countries celebrate their independence from their aggressors of old for a day or a week each year, the Republic of Panama has five different days off to commemorate independence during the month of November.

The dates of November 3, 4, 5, 10, and 28 are all celebrations of one event or another that brought liberty to the country. Here's the significance of each:

- November 3 – Separation (Independence) from Colombia
- November 4 – The Creation of the Panama flag
- November 5 – Celebrating a battle won in Colón (or when this particular town on the Atlantic coast stood up for itself against the Colombians)
- November 10 – In remembrance of the first battle cry in the Los Santos region in the battle against Spain
- November 28 – Independence from Spain

You can find a lot more information about all the holidays in Panama in the first book of the Gringo Guide to Panama series. However, it's important to note that the month of November is the beginning of the holiday *season* each year in this country.

Most Panamanians take the first week or the first two weeks of November for vacation, which covers November 3-5.

With another holiday off looming immediately afterward on November 10, people's minds visibly turn toward parties and barbeques, versus anything having to do with productivity.

This is hard to imagine until you experience it for yourself, but it's very much the case. It's difficult to get anything done in the month of November because every time you turn around, there's another holiday. And even when it's not a holiday, most locals are in the mindset of either reminiscing about one they just had, or focusing on what they'll doing when the *next* one rolls around.

Most expats find this roster of back-to-back holidays in November both intriguing and bewildering during their first year here. Then, they get frustrated when they experience the accompanying lack of motivation and increased inefficiency that pervades the country during the entire month.

The bottom line is that this holiday mindset in the month of November is the way it is in Panama, and you are not going to change it. Once you realize this, you'll go a long way toward finding enjoyment in this slower-than-usual paced month, versus feeling frustrated.

We found that it's best to plan that the month of November will not be a very productive one. You can expect about *half* the level of productivity from your staff or any service help in the course of business than in other months of the year. (Except for December, which is even *lower*, and I cover the reasons for that in the first book.)

But instead of getting frustrated, lighten up a little. Take advantage of the opportunity to take a few days off work.

Go to the beach. Relax at home. Go to the mall. During the holidays of November 3-5, we found that since most of the country heads to the beach, it's a great time to stay in the city. Traffic is non-existent, and you can get around very easily during these days, except for the time slots when parades are taking place. (Check the local papers for those.)

It simply helps your mental state-of-being as a Panama expat to expect less during November. When you have lower expectations of anything getting accomplished, you'll have a pleasant surprise when something actually does.

So, enjoy your Novembers in Panama, or at least plan that direction. When you've lived here for some time, this particular month might end up becoming one of the cultural aspects that you love most about the country.

North American Thanksgiving

In Panama, the Thanksgiving holiday is not a national holiday. This makes sense as the holiday is specific to the U.S., and not to anywhere else in the Americas. However, since there was a strong U.S. presence in the country with the U.S. operation of the Canal for the greater part of a century, most Panamanians are well aware of the holiday, though they may not personally celebrate it.

In 2008, we celebrated our first Thanksgiving holiday in Panama. (Like many other expats, we traveled back home to see family and friends about every other year during some part of the holiday season.) But in 2008, we had a hard time finding a restaurant that was serving the traditional

American Thanksgiving dinner of turkey, dressing, warm rolls, cranberry, pumpkin pie – the works.

Even in the local English speaking newspaper that year, there were no restaurants advertising for such a feast. We did finally locate one of the larger hotels – the Miramar Intercontinental Hotel on Avenida Balboa – and had our dinner there that year, buffet style with all the fixings.

Eight years later, you'll find many more options than we did in 2008 for your American Thanksgiving – at least in the city. On the beaches – especially in the Coronado area – check the local expat newspapers as well and you'll discover a few options as well. Most of the offerings should be listed in *The Visitor*, the only national expat newspaper offered in English.

Prefer to Cook?

Meanwhile, if you instead prefer to make your own Thanksgiving feast, where can you find everything you're looking for? We did that a few times. Below are a few resources that will help you pull it all together.

Fresh or Frozen?

First, the turkey. The key to finding your turkey is to do it as early as possible during the month, because you do have competition. Because not everyone celebrates, there's very limited supply. Turkey is not something you will find every day in most of the supermarkets during the rest of the year (unless you want turkey loaf or sliced turkey for sandwiches).

Finding a frozen turkey is your best bet, and most of the time, the three big supermarket chains will have them. But they won't be front and center when you go into the frozen section. Usually they are stuck back somewhere in a location that makes absolutely no sense, and may be hard to find. If so, grab a clerk to help you find them, and hope that your fellow expats haven't already purchased whatever limited supply they was shipped in.

For fresh turkeys, I'm only aware of one option, and that is Riba Smith, which is the nicest grocery in the city (and now open in Coronado on the Pacific coast). Check in at the meat counter several weeks in advance and inquire if you can get on the list for a fresh bird. Normally you will need to pick it up once they call and tell you it has arrived on either Monday or Tuesday the week of the holiday. (This process reminds me of my grandmother's era. If you didn't have access to a turkey farm back then, then your local grocer had to order one for you.)

Other grocery items which are not readily always available on your supermarket shelves and that you will find are more expensive include:

- Cranberries – normally, you'll have to buy these canned. I've never seen them fresh in Panama.
- Pumpkins – cost about ten times what they do in the U.S. In 2012, I priced a pumpkin for $24 in the supermarket. If you're on a budget, go for canned.
- Oysters – if these are a key ingredient in your stuffing recipe, you're going to have a hard time. The canned

variety are only occasionally available at Riba Smith, but don't count on it. You may wish to ask the market to order them several weeks in advance.

Wherever you find yourself in the country for Thanksgiving, you'll notice that you'll be greeted warmly by the local Panamanians with a *'Happy Thanksgiving!'* or *'Feliz Dia de Gracias'* wherever you go.

Part of the culture here is remembering and acknowledging other's birthdays and holidays with amazing consistency. This is a heartwarming tradition that every expat appreciates, especially when you're celebrating your holidays far from your home country.

Travel within the Country during Christmas

Many expats travel during the Christmas season to their home country to celebrate and visit family and friends. Panamanians do the same, but the bulk of their travel – unless they are well-to-do – is in-country, and most often to the *Interior*.

The Interior is defined as anywhere West of Panama City and past the city's two large suburbs, Arraijan and Chorrera, and stretching all the way to the Costa Rican border.

Mid-December marks the official start of summer in Panama. Kids get out of school for the year (unless they attend an international school, which follows a different calendar). As such, many families schedule their vacations from mid December to mid January. What this means for you, whether you've living in Panama or visiting Panama during this time period, is that the streets of the city are full of people, the traffic is never-ending, and the beaches fill up every weekend.

One of Panama's big draws is easy access to the beach. Contrary to what most people assume when they see photos of the city of Panama, there is no beach immediately in the city.

The closest public beach is in Veracruz – a 20-minute drive, across the Panama Canal, and south of the Panama Pacifico planned community. However, it's important to note that this beach is not a resort – it's a public beach popular with Panama's working class. On the weekends, Veracruz can get raucous and loud as it is home to a number of small locally-run *ranchos* that serve cold beer and fresh ceviche. It is the closest beach to the city for paddle boarding, however, so you'll find a number of paddle boarding providers there, renting boards, especially during the weekends. One of my favorite places for a workday lunch was to escape out the back gate of Panama Pacifico, the community adjacent to Veracruz, and enjoy some fresh fish, a cold Coca-Cola and some *patacones* at one of the local restaurants at Veracruz Beach. It's outdoor seating and can be very hot, but the fish is fresh and you can get a delicious plate lunch starting around $8. Karimar and Verimar are local favorites.)

Beaches on the Pacific Ocean can easily be reached within a 1-1.5 hour drive from the city, whereas those on the Caribbean are closer to 1.5-2 hours away. While the Caribbean is my favorite, most expats choose the Pacific side because it is more developed. The Pacific side has established hotels, more restaurants and better infrastructure, which make it easier and more convenient.

Beach Activity during December (and anytime)

Where do expats like to go on the Pacific side? For most, the stretch between Punta Chame and Buenaventura is the most popular. Punta Chame has become known for its unique beach geography, which offers one of the best areas in the region for kite surfing. It also has a NitroCity, which is big for all kinds of water sports, whether you're just out for the day or an entire weekend. NitroCity at Punta Chame is where Justin Bieber came to play when he visited the country a couple of years ago.

The beach community of Coronado looks and feels like a small suburb. This area has grown immensely in the past five years, now boasting numerous retail strip centers, with everything you could pretty much need for your beach stay (or if you live in the area): home improvement stores, clothing stores, beauty shops, vets, telecom providers, a hospital, pharmacies, surf shops, and even a casino.

The Coronado area is the top choice of North American expats who live full-time on Panama's Pacific coast. A number of our friends live here and like it. (If you're interested in renting or buying real estate in the Pacific beach area in Panama, I recommend speaking with Inside Panama Real Estate in Coronado. It's run by friendly U.S. expats, who have been living in Panama for several years, and they know their stuff. For vacation rentals, get in touch with my friend

Martha Vuytowecz at Inside Panama Management for excellent selection and service.

Coronado has a nice golf course, as well as a few gated communities, and quite a few restaurants. Panama's best liquor store – Felipe Motta – is also open in Coronado, bringing a wide variety of fine wines and beer to the area. Coronado's beach is long and flat, making it ideal for families with children and those learning to surf.

Beaches like Palmar, Gorgona, Corona, Santa Clara and Sea Cliff are more rustic. Most of these areas will have one or two hotels (if any), run by local families or establishments. The experience is simple and quiet.

Palmar is a good beach for beginning surfers. Gorgona is popular with middle-class locals and the younger crowd for a good raucous day party scene. Simple restaurants offer fresh fish, beverages, and hamburgers, but not much more. Day-trippers to these areas should plan to bring a lunch and their own drinks (if the simple fare mentioned is not of interest) – plus all their own beach gear – as there's not really any tourist facilities beyond what I've mentioned.

The most popular beaches for tourists – usually because travelers see their ads in the flight and hotel magazines – are Playa Blanca and the Decameron. These are your large, typical buffet-offering, lower-cost three-star resorts. At peak times, they resemble the Spring break beach party movies with cheap liquor flowing, swim-up bars, large pools, and loud groups. A lot of people come here for the inexpensive, all-you-can-eat, all-inclusive experience and they like it.

Further west, the Sheraton Hotel-Resort at Bijao offers a step up from the Decameron, with a condo community that includes a large, attractive beach club. Bijao also has a 9-hole golf course; neighboring Buenaventura has 18.

Buenaventura is the closest thing Panama has to offer akin to a true resort community. You can purchase real estate here ranging from a condo to a mansion, and enjoy the shared beach club, which is stock full of the well-heeled crowd on most weekends. Buenaventura also has a very nice hotel, which has already changed brands three times in the past five years, and is currently flying the JW Marriott brand. It's expensive, and I hear a lot of complaints about the food, but most people like the overall hotel.

Remember, You're Not in Costa Rica

It's important to know that what you'll find on Panama's Pacific coast is NOT at all the same as what you will find in Costa Rica. Costa Rica is 15-20 years ahead of Panama, in terms of their tourism infrastructure with four and five-star hotels and excellent service. Panama's experience is rustic, rural and growing. Don't expect much in terms of service. (Read the first book in the Gringo Guide to Panama series for more on that topic.)

Do go to the beaches in Panama with an open mind and look for true relaxation, and you'll find it. You will certainly find an adventure and simple beauty that has yet to be ruined by large development (at least in some places).

Eating in the Coronado area

Coronado has grown so much in the past few years that you can find almost every type of food in local restaurants. TripAdvisor will be your best bet online for the newest, latest reviews. Some lesser-known restaurants that have been open for years and are still serving good food follow.

- Cholo's (Coronado) – real Mexican fare, owned by a Mexican expat, open Wednesday through Sunday (usually)
- Los Camisones – fresh seafood and wonderful Paella
- Carlito's – simple pizza and empanadas in San Carlos
- The Bayview hotel restaurant in Palmar for a beach-front, rustic experience

10

LIVING IN PANAMA – EXPAT INTERVIEWS

The Casco Viejo (old city) coastline looking west

WHEN YOU ARE considering moving outside your native land, the best way to learn about a prospective country is to talk to other expats. Even after living in Panama for many years, I loved to hear other's stories, and what their experience has been. Every single person I talk to has an interesting story.

Those who come here choose different areas of the country. Some choose the city for work purposes. Others choose one of the beach areas. Many in search of a cooler climate prefer the mountains or slightly higher elevations.

In the pages that follow, you'll read a number of interviews with expats who live (or previously lived) in Panama in different areas. Each of these conversations took place in 2013. Each shared their own stories, perspectives and opinions about what life in Panama has looked like for them. Each of them proofread the written copy of their original interview to be sure the essence of the conversation was captured, and nothing had been missed or misinterpreted. (Some minor editing took place to fit the context of the book.)

All four of these particular people were ones I met through sharing my own stories about Panama via social media on Google Plus. (I never cease to be amazed at how technology these days connects us with new friends and acquaintances so quickly.)

I generally started with the same five questions when I interviewed them about their expat life. But because each person is unique, each interview usually takes a unique turn. I've tried to share four stories of people who came to Panama for different reasons: one who came to retire, one who came for lower costs of living, one who came in search of a different lifestyle, and one who came for more opportunity.

Please note that these interviews appear here in present tense in order to maintain their original integrity, as that's how they were published first on my Panama blog, www.PanamaGringoGuide.com.

Panama for Young Families:
Jennifer Luna

Photo courtesy of Jennifer Luna

One weekend earlier this year, I was leisurely reading *The Visitor*, Panama's English newspaper. Within it, I discovered a story about an expat with a cupcake business – Hola Cupcake – here in Panama. Since cupcakes bring out the kid in me (and hers were getting rave reviews), I got in touch to request an interview. Jennifer Luna graciously agreed, and soon after, I was fortunate enough to speak with her and to taste her culinary delights. I'm happy to report that hers are the *very* best cupcakes in Panama, and their popularity is growing.

But, baked goods were not really what brought Jennifer and her family to Panama. Read on for more of her story and what starting a business in Panama was like for her.

JuliAnne Murphy: Jennifer, first, I'm dying to know the origin of your last name – Luna. It sounds so mysterious. Where is it from?

Jennifer Luna: Actually, Luna is my married name. My husband is Panamanian.

JuliAnne: Okay, that probably answers the first question I had to ask you, which was what brought you to Panama?

Jennifer: (Laughs) Yes. You're right. I met my husband when we were in college at the University of Florida studying business. After graduation, we both found jobs in Tampa, Florida and lived there for eight years. He's in banking, and I was in property management. Our two children came very close together, just fourteen months apart. It's very difficult to have two small kids and two full-time jobs when you live in the States.

JuliAnne: I think it's hard no matter where you live, but yes, when you're in the States, it's a juggling act to have a balanced life with kids and full-time jobs. And most Americans can't afford a nanny or a full-time maid. So, what was it that your husband said that made you want to move here?

Jennifer: My husband kept telling me, "We can go to Panama and we can have a simpler life. You won't even have to work. We can afford help for the kids if we live there, like a nanny and a maid." Honestly, I took a lot of convincing before we made the decision to move. We were living very close to my parents in Florida, which I really enjoyed. But, we did make the move three years ago now, and we're very happy we came. Moving to Panama has been the best decision we've made.

JuliAnne: Jennifer, tell me a bit about you, your family, and some of your history. Had you been to Panama before, or lived outside the U.S. before you moved here?

Jennifer: I'm originally from Florida. I'd been to Europe on vacations – Italy, Paris, Mexico, but never to other places in Latin America. My husband and I had been coming to Panama for ten years to visit, usually for the New Year holiday. Every time we came here, I felt like at some point we'd move here, but I thought it would be during our retirement years, not when we had small kids.

I always saw how happy the retirees in Boquete seemed. We'd visited Boquete many times on our visits; we both fell in love with the area, and knew that we would want to be in Panama one day.

JuliAnne: Once you decided to move to Panama, what type of research did you do?

Jennifer: Because my husband is a native Panamanian, we already knew a lot. Actually, I think the first time I came to Panama with him was in 2001. Here's a photo of the Panama

City skyline from that very first trip we took (see below), which shows how much the city has grown since then.

Skyline of Panama in 2001 (courtesy of Jennifer Luna)

To answer your question about research, I did do a lot of research about the individual neighborhoods. Though we had visited before, I had never driven myself around in Panama. So once we decided to come, we planned a trip to come see the grandparents, and to look at different neighborhoods. We went out with a real estate agent. At first, I really wanted to live in Costa del Este – it felt more comfortable to me, more like a suburb in the U.S., easier to drive in, etc.

At that time, there were no high rises in Costa del Este, and all the new homes were just starting to be built, so it was kind of the newer area of town. But my husband really wanted to live in the city, because living in Costa del Este means you have a long commute. So we ended up in Punta Paitilla, which was an amazing choice for us. It's funny…my husband told me that when he was little, he used to drive through Paitilla and he always wanted to live there.

JuliAnne: Jennifer, how long was it from when you first started thinking about moving to Panama to when you actually relocated?

Jennifer: I believe it was 18 months. When we first started thinking about it, my son was about six months old and we moved when he was two.

JuliAnne: When I first contacted you a few weeks ago, you mentioned you were moving. Did you stay in the Paitilla neighborhood, or did you choose another area within the city?

Jennifer: We just moved to San Francisco near Parque Omar (one of Panama's large parks). With the kids getting bigger, it made sense for them to be able to ride bikes nearby. We loved Paitilla, but we felt we needed more outdoor space.

JuliAnne: What has been a surprise for you – living in Panama as an expat – now that you have been here for three years?

Jennifer: The biggest surprise was the number of people I found here that speak English. When we visited Panama for vacation, we were always around Spanish speakers, most of whom were my husband's family and friends. I was always trying to keep up with them speaking Spanish (and knowing very little myself). Unfortunately, because a lot of people speak English in Panama, it can make it really hard to learn Spanish.

JuliAnne: How is your Spanish? Are you fluent after three years?

Jennifer: I can read almost everything. I can understand about 75% of what people say, except for the slang. If there's a big group talking rapidly in Spanish, I have a hard time following the conversation.

JuliAnne: Since you'd visited Panama several times before you moved here, what was different than what you originally thought it might be?

Jennifer: Well, my husband had lived in the U.S. for some time before we came back, so it was actually a surprise to both of us at how the technology is still a bit behind. Neither of us expected the inefficiencies we encounter, still today, in a country that's growing so quickly. This was a big shocker coming from the U.S., where everything is so efficient, not just in simple tasks, but for scheduling things. Here in Panama, people don't always show up when they are supposed to, nor do they call if they can't make the appointment. That's a good thing for people to know when they are moving here.

One of my friends was the first resident to occupy a brand new apartment in the Punta Pacifica (luxury) neighborhood. When things have to be fixed here, it often takes multiple trips and workers coming in and out of your personal space for months to get the job done. This was the case for her with their new apartment during their first year here. That experience really ruined Panama for her. They ended up leaving the country as a result.

With our recent move, I tried to be realistic with my own expectations about getting settled in, and things getting done (in a timely fashion).

JuliAnne: So, let's get down to your cupcake business – aptly called *Hola* Cupcake – I've heard they are yummy! (*Hola* means *hello* or *hi* in Spanish.) How did you get started?

Jennifer: We had been living in Panama about 6-7 months when my sister-in-law also moved here. She was not working at the time. My sister had sent me a *Hello Cupcake!* book for making cupcakes with fun candies and different recipes. (Note: *Hello, Cupcake!* is a New York Times bestselling cookbook for irresistibly playful creations that anyone can make, according to their website.) Remember that movie – *Julie and Julia* – about a gal who cooked Julia Child's recipes every day for a year and blogged about it?

JuliAnne: Oh, yes! I loved that movie.

149

Jennifer: Well, that movie inspired me. So, I decided to do a blog with cupcakes from the *Hello Cupcake!* cookbook. But our first batch, which we did at Christmas two years ago, was horrible. They all melted because of the heat. Then my sister-in-law got a job (and could not help me any longer).

My husband had a Christmas party at his office and asked me to make my grandmother's carrot cake. So I did and he took it to the party. Well, he came back with glowing compliments, and several of his staff asked if I might consider making carrot cakes for their holiday celebrations.

JuliAnne: That must be some recipe!

Jennifer: Yes, well…EIGHT cakes later, they all came back from their holiday celebrations, and were asking for what else I made. So, that was the beginning.

I created a menu based on my mom's cookbook. She has a recipe for a buttercream icing that does not melt, and I used that to make a menu of flavors. My husband took the cupcake menu back to his office, and the word spread.

That was two years ago. Now I don't really know where my clients come from; I just keep getting calls. Soon after, I started my Facebook page, and took photos of the cakes and the cupcakes, so people can see them online.

I have 18 cupcake flavors on the menu, and a few other things too: an Oreo truffle, shortbread cookies, marshmallow pops, and brownies. But my preference is to make cupcakes; those are my favorite.

Jennifer's cupcakes from Hola Cupcake

JuliAnne: Jennifer, do you run Hola Cupcake full-time? And do you have a retail location, or operate out of your home?

Jennifer: At the moment, my operation is part-time, and I bake from home. I bake three or four times a week, and only when someone orders. My kids are four and five years old and have afternoon activities. They're really my priority.

JuliAnne: Understood. They're why you came to Panama after all. Do you do any marketing at all for your business? Cupcakes have been the rage now in the U.S. for several years but they're just now really hitting Panama. How do people find you?

Jennifer: I really don't do any marketing except for social media. Most of my clients come from word of mouth. Even the article in *The Visitor* that you read came about from word of mouth. I baked cupcakes for the editor's birthday and his office loved them, so they did a story. If I choose to market more than what I do now, I might get overwhelmed and then I'd have to get more serious. I'm not ready for that yet.

JuliAnne: Jennifer, I get asked a lot about what it's like to be an entrepreneur in Panama. Are there any ups and downs you'd to share in terms of what it takes to get started here?

Jennifer: Honestly, you just have to be patient with the processes of Panama, in terms of getting your work Visa. It was easier for me, given that my husband is Panamanian. But because of how inefficient some of the processes here can be, it can be stressful. So I'd say, just be patient.

JuliAnne: What are your top three recommendations for new expats considering Panama?

Jennifer:
1. I recommend visiting Panama more than two times before you decide to move here permanently, and to stay an extended amount of time. There are plenty of places you can rent for a month. I've heard a lot of stories of those who have jumped in too quickly, and have not found Panama to be a fit.
2. The best thing that happened to me after I moved here was meeting another English-speaking mom in the park with my kids. We struck up a conversation. Through her,

I met a mommy group, which literally changed my overall experience of the country. So that's my second recommendation: Find a connection for yourself, especially with other English speakers.

3. Get out of the city when you can. Go to Boquete, Pedasi, San Blas, the Pearl Islands, etc. In Panama, you can travel from the Atlantic to the Pacific within two hours. It's important to get out and explore the beautiful country, because it has a little bit of everything.

JuliAnne: Great advice, Jennifer! Thanks so much for sharing your story, and that of your business – Hola Cupcake. It's exciting to hear that Panama has become a great fit for you and your young family, and also that Panama is embracing your cupcakes!

For more on Hola Cupcake, visit their Facebook page (www.facebook.com/holacupcakepty), or contact Jennifer for a menu locally here in Panama at +507-6920-0958 or email her at holacupcakepty@gmail.com.

Jennifer was kind enough soon after this interview to send me a batch of her cupcakes. Take it from me: these are the best darn cupcakes in the country! I highly, highly recommend them. It's no wonder Hola Cupcake stays as busy as it does without any advertising.

Panama for Affordability:
Susanna Perkins

Photo courtesy of Susanna Perkins

Susanna Perkins celebrated her first year of living in Panama in March 2013. She and her husband moved from Orlando, Florida to Las Tablas, a small town in Panama's Interior, in March 2012. While her husband is retired, Susanna works full-time in her own online businesses. One is Future Expats Forum, which she began to chronicle their process of moving abroad in 2009. The other is WordPress Building Blocks, which helps non-technical people get educated about building their own websites.

JuliAnne: Susanna, why did you choose Panama as your new country?

Susanna Perkins: First of all, thanks for the opportunity to speak with you. When people ask me that question, my reply is '*Do as I say, not as I do.*' The short answer is that we were whacked by the economic meltdown in the U.S. in 2009. We were interested in a more affordable lifestyle, one where we could actually live comfortably on our income. We wanted to stay close to the U.S., so we could travel easily to see our grown children. After a lot of evaluation, we narrowed our list to three countries: Mexico, Ecuador and Panama.

Mexico fell off the list due to a comment one of our daughters made that she would not feel safe visiting us there. My husband worked with a colleague who did some business in Panama, so his comfort level with Panama became higher over time, as he heard more and more about it.

JuliAnne: Over what period of time did your research take place? Months? Years?

Susanna: We had been thinking about retiring abroad for several years. I would say probably six years from start to finish. We got serious about planning for the actual move between the years of 2009 and 2012.

JuliAnne: What resources did you find useful that you might recommend to others considering a similar move?

Susanna: I had done a lot of looking around online, and of course, I found International Living. Once we narrowed our list down to Panama, I discovered some online forums, which were helpful. Kathleen Peddicord had started Live &

Invest Overseas, and I received their subscription service. I also attended a conference of theirs here in Panama for three days, which was key for us. After the conference ended, my husband joined me for a weeklong tour of the country. What we found most helpful was talking to other expats.

JuliAnne: Was the week you came to look around sufficient before making the decision to move? Would you recommend anything different to others?

Susanna: If someone can afford to spend longer than a week then I recommend it. Our budget allowed us a week so we had to make it work.

JuliAnne: Susanna, you moved here with your husband and your three dogs. Why did you choose Las Tablas versus the city of Panama or some of the other areas that many expats are drawn to, such as Coronado or Boquete?

Susanna: When we came for our week visit, we spent three days in Panama City, three days in David, then went to Boquete and Las Tablas. As soon as we pulled into town, we really liked Las Tablas. It's a small town, and it feels manageable, plus it's attractive and lively. We both felt comfortable here. We'd actually planned to go on to Penonome for the final leg of our journey, but we liked Las Tablas so much that we canceled that part of the trip.

JuliAnne: I've been through Las Tablas a few times enroute to Pedasi and Venao. Tell me more about what you found appealing about the area.

The church in the town square in Las Tablas

Susanna: While Las Tablas has a population of about 10,000 people, it serves the region around it in terms of retail and shopping. We have two good size groceries, and a new supermarket under construction. There are plenty of small clothing, housewares, electronics, and furniture stores. You can find a lot of what you need right here in town. If there's something you need beyond what's available here, you can probably find it in nearby Chitre. Las Tablas has quite a few restaurants ranging from small local cafes to some nicer places. While there's not a huge variety in terms of types of food, you do have some choices.

Las Tablas is also in a drier part of Panama (meaning it gets less rain), which makes it less humid than some other areas, and we liked that.

There are three local hotels (though no chains) and a nice downtown park with free WiFi.

JuliAnne: Wow! Free WiFi in a park? Not even Panama City has that at the moment!

Susanna: We've also found a really good vet here, which was important because we brought our three dogs with us, as I mentioned.

JuliAnne: You said that you were looking for a place where you could live more affordably (than in the U.S.). Have you found that in Las Tablas?

Susanna: Actually, the cost of living when we moved here turned out to be a bit more than we expected. We were basing our expectations on what we had seen when we did our weeklong visit here in 2011. Prices on housing and food had increased about 30% from 2011 to 2012, which was significant. But, at the same time, we are now living within our budget, and that's what we set out to do. I have done a cost of living analysis on my website, and if anyone's interested, they can take a look at that.

JuliAnne: Susanna, do you or your husband speak Spanish?

Susanna: We don't speak much. I studied for a couple of semesters at a community college before we moved to Panama. Sometimes, I get frustrated when I can't communicate clearly because of the language barrier, but I'm better than I was when we arrived a year ago. With what we've learned, we can conduct basic day-to-day business in our limited Spanish. If we have an emergency, we call on a couple of local bilingual friends.

JuliAnne: What has been the most surprising aspect of life in Panama for the two of you?

Susanna: Two things come to mind. I thought it would be easier to find someone to take care of our dogs in our home, for when we travel, like a pet sitter. We used a pet sitter when we lived in the U.S., but have not been able to find that type of service here in Panama. There is a local vet who will board our dogs at his house, but pet sitting services *per se* don't really exist here yet. Part of that may be because the attitude about pets here is different than it is in the U.S.

Second, I had read about the fact that Panamanians love to party, get rowdy and play their music loudly on the weekends. This doesn't necessarily bother me, but the type of music that's commonly played here has taken some getting used to (for me).

My husband gets really upset at the roadside litter we encounter here. He goes out a couple of times a week and picks up trash on the side of the road or at the beach. I remind him that everyone littered in the U.S. too, back in the 60's and 70's.

JuliAnne: You're right. Remember the government campaigns of *Give a Hoot, Don't Pollute!* and *Keep America Beautiful?* Panama has recently begun a grass-roots campaign against littering. The reality is that it's probably going to take years for that to take hold. Most expats I talk to have a hard time with the trash.

Susanna: The nicest thing about Panama is the people. Our fellow citizens in Las Tablas have been so kind to us. They're warm and friendly, and we've been treated really well. This has been a really nice surprise and another reason why Panama has been the right choice for us.

A very special thanks to Susanna Perkins for her willingness to share. If you are semi-retired or considering the Interior area, especially the Azuero coast, connect with Susanna via Google+ or on her websites and read more of her stories.

Panama for Young Expats:
Skyler Ralston

Photo courtesy of Skyler Ralston

In recent years, I've seen an increase in the number of younger people looking at Panama – those younger than 40. Often they are being recruited for a job here. Other times, they have some kind of a link to Panama – their parents retired here, or they've vacationed here several times.

Many of this age group, often referred to as the Millenials, are looking for a different lifestyle from previous generations. I hear from many of them that their priorities are different: they want to escape the typical corporate grind.

Skyler Ralston's story falls into two of these categories. Her parents retired to Panama several years ago, and she was interested in something other than the corporate scene she'd experienced in her first few years in the workforce.

Skyler is in her late 20s. Originally hailing from Boston, she'd visited Panama multiple times to see her parents, and she liked it. In December 2009, after working in advertising for two years in Miami, she decided to come to Panama and try it out.

JuliAnne: Skyler, I've heard your name many times over the past two years. Tell me what was it that brought you to Panama originally.

Skyler Ralston: Hi! I'm happy to be chatting with you. My degree is in marketing and international business with a minor in Spanish. I've always been interested in Spanish and Latin culture because my grandfather is Chilean. As my parents are very adventurous, I had already lived in three other countries – Costa Rica, Spain and Chile – before I came to Panama.

JuliAnne: What kind of business do you do?

Skyler: I'm an entrepreneur. I have two ventures: One, an association called YEP! which stands for *Young Expats in Panama*, and two, a marketing firm called Sky Marketing (www.skymarketingpanama.com).

JuliAnne: I've heard a lot about YEP in the past year or so. Tell me more about it.

Skyler: YEP! is a super fun networking group connecting like-minded internationals and global minded Panamanians at Panama's hottest locations.

Courtesy of YEP

I started YEP! in 2011. (The two year anniversary was in August 2013.) When I moved here, I didn't know anyone other than my parents. I searched for something like YEP! – a young people's organization or group, or a way to connect with young people in Panama, and I found nothing. I wanted to meet people and make friends.

After I'd been here a year, I had met some people, but I knew there had to be more young expats like me, and I wanted to connect with them. Since no kind of club or social group existed that focused on fun exchanges, I decided to start one. That's how YEP! came to be.

JuliAnne: YEP! has obviously been very successful, Skyler. I've read the media coverage of some of your events and seen ads and announcements of upcoming activities in the newspaper here and there. It looks like you guys have fun!

Skyler: We do have fun. The funny thing is that YEP! has turned into a business, which was never my intention. When I started it, I had no idea how much time and effort would be involved in putting together the kinds of events we do.

JuliAnne: Is there an age limit on YEP?

Skyler: YEP! is aimed at the young expats in Panama – usually between 25-35 years old – many of whom are working in multinational companies. Some are entrepreneurs like myself and others are more of the backpacking crowd – working for a non-profit or the Peace Corp. There's no age limit. We say YEP! is for the young in age or the young at heart.

JuliAnne: Are most of your attendees to the YEP! events from the U.S.?

Skyler: Primarily from the U.S. and Canada, yes. But as YEP! has become more well-known, more Panamanians have started coming to the events. This has been really exciting, as I had previously found some of the locals difficult to socialize with. (They seemed to stay in their own cliques.) I found that many were now coming to YEP! events for one of three reasons: they had studied abroad, they spoke English and wanted to practice, or they were trying to learn English. Because YEP! has become so popular with Panamanians too, we've updated our slogan. It's now *Meet Global Minded Panamanians.*

JuliAnne: Talk more about the events YEP! offers.

Skyler: The focus of YEP! is getting together to have fun. My goal was to offer fun events and activities so that people can connect and socialize. Some of the things we've done in the past include day trips to Nitro City Panama Actions Sports Resort, poker tournaments, cocktail cruises, themed parties, wine tastings, etc.

We're establishing an annual calendar on the website, so that people can mark the dates of the ones they want to attend. We have big events like a big one a couple of weeks ago at Hard Rock Hotel, which hosted 250 people. Then, there are smaller, more intimate events like wine tastings and day trips to the beach, with a max of 30 attendees.

We usually host two events each month. The venues change all the time, as well as the themes. Sometimes the events are free; sometimes there's a fee up to $15, which includes two hours of an open bar. I try to offer attendees the best bang for their buck and their time, and also give them a unique experience.

A flyer from one of YEP!'s 2013 events (courtesy of Skyler)

The big event I mentioned was called YEP! Top of the Rock party at Hard Rock Hotel. The theme was a black and silver party. The teaser was: *Be shimmery in silver. Be bold in black. An evening of elegance under the stars.* This particular event was sponsored by Ketel One Vodka, so there were specials on Ketel One vodka and martinis all night. *Revista Weekend* magazine with La Prensa covered the event.

JuliAnne: Skyler, any idea how many young expats there are in Panama?

Skyler: Not really, but I can tell you that there are hundreds. We get 300+ attendees coming to the bigger YEP! events.

JuliAnne: What other resources does the group offer for young people in Panama?

Skyler: I get so many questions about the different parts of the city of Panama (for living) that I put together a summary of the neighborhoods. You can find that on the website. (Note though that it is from a young person's point of view.)

Also, similar to what you did with the Gringo Guide to Panama, I put together some helpful tips, which I titled the *Real Deal Panama*. That's really good for when you're new to town.

There's also a Help Desk forum on the website. I get emails all the time from job seekers and from firms looking to hire English speakers. In the future, you'll see job listings here, and you'll be able to post your resume there too.

Lastly, we are compiling premium discount vouchers to Panama's top businesses exclusively for the YEP! group in the Savings/Rewards section of the website. (At the time of the interview, for example, the Savings featured half price entry to Isabella Disco & Lounge on Friday nights, and 75% off language learning at Bristol Academy.) We're also using QR codes so it's more sustainable and green.

JuliAnne: What type of impact has YEP! had on your own personal experience of living in Panama?

Skyler: I always had the goal of owning my own marketing company. That's possible for me in Panama, whereas it might not be in the U.S. at this young age, if I were back in Boston or Miami. Putting on the events for YEP! has become fuel for my marketing business – Sky Marketing – which has been really exciting.

YEP! has also been an outlet for me to make friends. I've also discovered new things about Panama from others who have been here longer than me, along the way. Now, two years later, it's rewarding to connect and help others based on what I've learned.

JuliAnne: Skyler, was there anything about Panama that was a surprise for you, once you moved here to live?

Skyler: There are big differences from when you come to visit, versus when you move here. For example, driving in Panama is like nothing I've ever seen. When I first arrived, the traffic terrified me. I can certainly hold my own on the road now, versus when I first arrived, but it took a while.

JuliAnne: After having lived here for so many years, you kind of have to sink or swim when it comes to the driving culture here. I always have to remind my husband – *"Stop driving like a Panamanian! You're going to get arrested!"* – when we go back to visit the States, and he's zooming around other cars and cutting people off.

Skyler: Another surprise for me here was the relaxed pace. I've lived in three other Spanish-speaking countries, and even so, I never encountered what I call the *tropical mentality* like I've seen here. I've really had to learn patience since I moved here – both with the slower pace and the inefficiency.

JuliAnne: Do you have any observations about Panama as it compares to the U.S.?

Skyler: I would say that Panama is five to seven years behind the U.S. It has its flaws and its development challenges, but it also has unbelievable opportunity. It's really exciting to be here at this point – launching my business and seeing it grow – and I'm excited to see how Panama will change and grow in the next five years.

JuliAnne: What types of things do you do for fun or on the weekends apart from YEP!?

Skyler: I love to travel. My policy is to leave Panama City at least every few weeks. We're so close to world-renowned beaches here in Panama. I love San Blas (which is located on the Atlantic side) and staying in a hut or a tent, where a cellphone does not work. I enjoy totally disconnecting and hanging with my dog and my friends.

JuliAnne: Skyler, Panama is known for a pretty active night-life for younger people. Any comments on that?

Skyler: Panama has a pretty cool gambling scene if you're into poker. And, yes, there's tons of nightlife activity, almost any type of scene you want. You just have to get out and explore. I used to be an avid poker player. When I first came to Panama, I was playing up to three nights a week in some of the local casinos. That slowed down a bit though once I got YEP! up and running. (Note: Gambling in Panama is legal. See Chapter 13 for more on casinos in Panama.)

JuliAnne: How is Panama different for people younger than 40 years old?

Skyler: Older people (40+) in Panama are usually more established in their lives, in their careers, with families, etc. I've found that the 25-35 age group is all about getting out and enjoying the city. We're more footloose and fancy free, if you will – going out, having cocktails, experiencing the nightlife.

JuliAnne: What are your top three recommendations for younger people moving (or considering moving) to Panama?

Skyler: I actually get asked that question all the time: do you recommend Panama for younger people? Here's what I recommend.

First, join YEP! and come to every group event. I love to meet everyone and hear their stories. Being a part of YEP! is a good way to get comfortable with the country. It makes you feel more at home when you meet other English speakers and especially those in your own age group that know Panama.

Second, get out of the city and travel. Be adventurous! I'm not into camping generally but now one of my favorite getaways, as I said, is to sleep under the stars on the beach in San Blas.

Third, experience the diversity that Panama has to offer – from top nightlife spots to private deserted beaches…there's so much here that can't be accessed anywhere else in the world. I encourage people to take advantage of that.

JuliAnne: Every country has its faults. What are the things you're not so fond of here in Panama, or what things do you miss about the U.S.?

Skyler: Well, there's no Target and Wal-Mart here, so I stock up on my necessities from places like that when I travel back.

I miss the ease of how certain things are done in the U.S. versus here. For example, in the U.S., I can walk into a cell phone store and get something done to my phone in ten minutes. A similar fix to my cell phone here in Panama recently took eight trips and two months from start to finish, and that drove me crazy. It could be so much more efficient but at times, it's just not, and that can cause you a lot of stress. So, now I just plan for the fact that things will take much longer.

Standing in line in Panama is almost a national pastime

JuliAnne: (Laughing) Yes, that's one of Panama's big realities. I wrote quite a bit about that in my first book, the original Gringo Guide to Panama: What to Know Before You Go. Anything else?

Skyler: I never thought I'd miss the U.S. mail system or that I would take online shopping for granted. But here, I've kind of forgotten what online shopping is. The import taxes alone cost so much that it's not worth shipping things in, so it's not something I do very often anymore.

JuliAnne: Amen! It's called taking an extra suitcase back when you go, right? I always do that. Skyler, tell me about an experience you might never have had if you had not moved to Panama.

Skyler: Starting my company, Sky Marketing, at such a young age is something I would not have been able to do elsewhere. That, and the success I've already enjoyed with it.

JuliAnne: Tell me more about what you mean by that.

Skyler: I never thought I would be in the position I am now – with two successful companies – at such a young age. Obviously, that success has not come without a lot of hard work. But a few weeks ago, I had to stop and kind of pinch myself. I realized that in just one week, I had met with top executives of each of the top five hotels in Panama. I realize how impressive that was, but it's due to the connections I've made and to the work I've done here in Panama. It's cool for me to appreciate how far I've come as a professional in my few years here.

JuliAnne: Skyler, your story is so inspiring, and the YEP! group is really something. Kudos to you on your own success, as well as that of YEP!

A special thanks to Skyler Ralston for her time and her excitement in sharing her experiences of life in Panama.

Take note of how to get in touch with YEP! in social media.

Twitter:
@YoungExpatsinPA
twitter.com/YoungExpatsinPA
@FiestasPanama
twitter.com/FiestasPANAMA

Facebook:
facebook.com/YoungExpatsinPanama

Facebook Group:
facebook.com/groups/youngexpatsinpanama/

The best way for anyone to stay current with where the YEP! action is taking place is to sign up for the subscriber database on the homepage of their website:

www.youngexpatsinpanama.com

Panama for Retirees:
Jackie Smith

Photo courtesy of Jackie Smith

Jackie Smith and her husband Mike moved to Panama in October 2012. Their plan was to stay with friends who reside in Boquete for a period of six months in Panama's western Interior in order to get a feel for Panama. Jackie and I met on Google+, and she was kind enough to be interviewed about their experiences in finding Panama, moving to Panama, and what life in Panama has been for them.

JuliAnne: Jackie, why did you move to Panama originally? What led you to choose to come here?

Jackie Smith: We have friends who have lived in Boquete for 10 years. They told us for many years how much they love Panama. Last year, the time was right for us to look at the country for ourselves, and see if we could make it our home.

We actually have always wanted to move to Cyprus, an island in the eastern Mediterranean. My husband and I lived there before, on military posts, and also, when we worked for a large British tour operator. Unfortunately, the economic situation in Europe has made living there impossible for us, as the cost of living is too high.

JuliAnne: Do you currently work, or are you retired? If you work, what type of work do you do?

Jackie: We're effectively retired, though we are younger than the 'usual' retirement age. My husband Mike receives a military pension, and we have rental properties in the U.K. At the end of 2011, Mike was offered early retirement at the university where he worked. Around the same time, I left my job at a major bank. We went to Thailand for the first six months of 2012 to see if we might like to live there, but we decided it wasn't for us. Now we're here, and will live here for six months to see if maybe Panama is more to our liking.

JuliAnne: Did you do any research about Panama before you came?

Jackie: We had been to Panama in 2003 after our friends moved here. Since then, we've kept an eye on the country. It's had so many consistent positive ratings as a great place to live, and it's been consistently praised as a number one place for retirees. So, really our research was ongoing over a period of many years.

JuliAnne: What were the factors that led you to choose Boquete?

Jackie: We really came here because our friends were here. In the months since we've lived in Panama, we've visited other areas – the beach, Panama City, etc. – but we enjoy the cooler climate in Boquete. The beach area is beautiful, but it's too hot for us. We also figured our utility costs would be higher in the city of Panama because you might use year-round air conditioning. Here in Boquete, we've used absolutely no heating or cooling systems at all. We live in shorts, and only on occasion, even need a sweater.

JuliAnne: Have there been any aspects of Panama that surprised you?

Jackie: We are blown away by the friendliness of the Panamanian people. Everywhere we go there are smiles – in shops, bars, and restaurants. We feel very welcome here. When we've needed something, people have bent over backwards to help us.

JuliAnne: Is there anything you would do differently in preparing to move, or in evaluating a move to Panama, if you could do it over again?

Jackie: Honestly, no. I don't feel we would have done anything differently than we did.

JuliAnne: What are the things you really like about Panama?

Jackie: I have a list! I really like the food. I like the fact that you can be at the beach for lunch on Sunday. Then, if you fancy a change that same day, you can take a hike up into the rainforest because it's right next door.

I love the consistent climate and the beauty of Boquete. I love photography, and I am overwhelmed by all the beauty here – the birds, the flowers, a stunning rainbow here, a crystal clear waterfall there.

We really love the cheaper cost of living. You can buy local products instead of brand name imports and save a lot of money. However, I do like having the choice of purchasing more expensive high-end stuff if I want it. I have never felt as though I am missing something from home.

I love the fact that Panama is so central to North America, South America, and the Caribbean Islands. You don't have to travel far or at too great an expense to see another country.

JuliAnne: I've heard comments from some expats that life in Boquete can be too quiet...even boring...because it's so small. What's your experience been?

Jackie: To keep ourselves occupied, we have started a blog to document our experience of life in Boquete. (You can take a look at it at www.bellaboquete.info.)

Like you, it seems sensible to share what we are learning as we go along so that others can benefit from our research, if they are looking to make the move here. We're hoping eventually to turn the blog into an income-producing vehicle, and maybe even write a book in the future based on our experiences.

JuliAnne: There's no doubt that the more information people have, the better, before making such an important life change. So, thank you again for being willing to share about what it has been like for you, Jackie. Do you and your husband plan to stay in Panama permanently, or are you just here for a set amount of time?

Jackie: Currently, our thoughts are to stay permanently, with no plans to return to Britain. The cost of living is too high there, and we prefer this climate. We will maintain a base there though, just in case we decide to return.

In July 2013, I saw a note from Jackie on Google+ that she and her husband had left Panama, and did not plan to return.

Naturally, this piqued my interest so I wrote her for a follow-up interview. Obviously something had changed from our prior conversation. The reasons behind their decision not to return will be as interesting for anyone who does decide to make Panama their permanent home. Here's what she told me via email.

Jackie: Thanks for getting in touch. I completely understand why you'd want to learn more about what led to our departure. We loved Panama. It is a wonderful country, and we totally loved being in Boquete. We really fell in love with the nature, the rain forest, the people, and of course, the beaches are to die for. But here are our overall thoughts:

- For us, as Europeans, living in Panama was too far from home and family. We found the travel cost for plane tickets alone to be prohibitively expensive.
- Boquete was too small for our tastes. Panama City was too hot.
- We loved the idea of visiting the country, but within the first six months, we learned that we did not want to make Panama our permanent home, despite all the wonderful things the country has to offer.
- In Boquete, the Internet drove us crazy...it is *soooo* slow. If you ran your business online, it could be very frustrating. Even Skype calls became difficult to make and to depend on because of the internet speed.
- In Boquete, we found the mobile/cell phone reception to be terrible.

Now (in August 2013), my husband and I are regrouping. I am back at work full-time again so that we can finance a new plan. Our time in Panama (because it was not the first foreign country evaluation we'd done) did help us clarify a few things. We've realized that we are not destined to live in just one place.

As I mentioned in our prior interview, my husband and I lived in Cyprus before and really liked it. Over time, we realized we both wanted to go back to Cyprus and that desire has not changed for either of us. So, we've decided to live there part of the year, though perhaps not permanently. (I do run a travel site about this island, which I have had for some time (www.the-real-cyprus.com), and I have been approached by a travel company in Kuwait to do some writing for their magazine about the island.)

My husband and I plan to buy a caravan and a four-wheel drive vehicle in early 2014, so we can travel all over the U.K., visit Europe, and more or less stop wherever and whenever we want to...to satisfy our wanderlust.

Since we came back to the U.K. a few weeks ago, we're received medical results which indicate that my husband needs to have both his hips replaced. We're both grateful to be able to use the National Health system in the U.K., because paying for this in Panama would have been difficult for us.

My top tip for any retiree is this. Even if you have visited Panama on short trips many times, it's best to rent a place for six months to a year before you *completely* decide to move.

Do this before you give up anything in your home country. This will allow you time to *really* be sure you like it, because it may not be how you think it is. Two weeks here and there does not give you a realistic feel for how things will be once you live here.

(Author note: I personally do not care much for Boquete. My husband and I visited for a long weekend several years ago, and our experience was that the social expat scene there is very clique-ish, pretty gossipy and very small. While the natural setting is spectacular, if Boquete is on your list, I encourage you to spend a good amount of time there before you make an investment to make sure it's to your personal liking.)

Special thanks to Jackie (and her husband Mike, though I have not had the pleasure of meeting him) for their openness, and willingness to share about their experiences in Panama, and the unvarnished truth of what led them to decide the country was *not* the right fit for them.

11

YOU KNOW YOU'RE IN
PANAMA WHEN...

The prevalence of roadside trash is one of the country's ugly traits

ONCE IN A while, every expat in Panama has what I call a 'bad Panama day'. A day when everything irks you, and all the idiosyncracies of the country rub you the wrong way. These occasions were the ones when I yearned to run back to civilization (in the U.S.) and lose myself at SuperTarget, with a Starbucks in hand. These were the reveries I called my "island escapes" when I lived in Panama.

In 2015, Starbucks came to Panama, so for those that live in the city, that part of my "island escape" is now accessible.

But the U.S. life of convenience and comfort and normalcy was not the one we chose - my husband and I - in the years we lived in Panama together. Instead, we chose adventure. We chose this quirky little country. So, on the days I needed a break from the adventure we called expat life, I crafted a list of funny Panama things. It's not quite Saturday Night Live, but…well, read on.

A Top Ten list of Local Idiosyncrasies

Each of these are best framed when you put the phrase, "You know you're in Panama …." in front of each.

- When it's not necessary to pull off the road when a police car comes up behind you with flashing lights. Nope, just keep driving. You can also pass a police car here, without fear.
- When you see the local ladies walking down the street with their umbrellas to shade themselves from the sun. It's a strange sight for a few years, then somehow it becomes cute.
- When the workers who swore they would arrive no later than 6:30 a.m. show up closer to 10 a.m., without apology. (And never mind that you came in specifically to meet them, so the work would not impact your co-workers or your clients. Never mind that. That's really your problem.)
- When your favorite employee comes to work wearing 6-inch heels and you don't even give them a second

thought. (Nor do you any longer think something along the lines of, "Is she hopping a flight to Vegas?")

- When every resume you receive has a sexy headshot of the applicant on it. (Aren't real estate brokers the only ones that do this in the U.S.?) In Panama, including your picture on your resume or job application is the norm, even for professional positions.

- When you wait and *wait* and wait outside the closed bathroom door at your office, assuming someone's in there, only to realize five minutes later than no one actually *is*. (It's a cultural habit to keep the door *closed* in Panama when the bathroom is vacant, versus leaving it open to let the next inhabitant know that no one is in it (like we do in the U.S.). It took me a very long while to get the hang of this.

- When your fellow passengers crowd the luggage carousels so closely that you can't peer between them to spot your bag coming around (at the airport)... until it's already passed you by. Then you have to push through the crowd to get it (which seems rude) or wait until it comes all the way around again.

- When you no longer bat an eye when your fellow female co-worker snorts loudly during a business meeting, repeatedly. Granted, she has a cold, but loud snorting, for any reason, in this culture is generally acceptable and not considered at all unusual or *feo* (an ugly trait).

185

Getting cut-off in traffic is the norm here

- When people circle and circle and circle (and circle…) in their cars in the front part of the parking lot to find a parking place for 30 minutes, instead of taking one a little further back that will require a two-minute walk. (Sometimes it seems that Panamanians hate to walk anywhere.)
- When the front desk personnel at the hotel where your event is being held tells all the incoming attendees that there's no event by that name, when the door to the event is just around the corner from the hotel's front desk. Sigh. This is Panama.

Living in Panama as a foreigner requires a great deal of flexibility, patience and most importantly, a good sense of humor. Opportunities abound every single day to learn, to appreciate, and to laugh. When frustration hits, which it *will*, refer back to your copy of the first book in the Gringo

Guide to Panama series to chuckle or read more of these types of *living in Panama* realities.

At least, you'll be able to laugh along the way.

12

GETTING YOURSELF MOVED

Old buildings next to new ones in Casco Viejo

Y OU'VE JUST SOLIDIFIED your work contract for your new job in Panama. Now what? You're bringing your spouse. You need a place to live. You have kids who need a school. Where to begin? Maybe you're moving to Panama to retire, or to make your money go further. Whatever brings you, you'll find that the process of moving internationally is much more involved than an interstate one.

One of Life's Most Stressful Events

First things first. If you are a professional, ask your company if they are providing a relocation service company to assist you in your plan for moving to Panama. If they are not, get a quote from a relocation company physically located in Panama to help you with all the legwork on this end. It will make your life much simpler.

Next, make a list. What are all the immediate things you need to do to give your plan some shape so that it doesn't feel so overwhelming? Getting everything down on paper usually helps create a sense of order. Plus, it empties the mind of all the things you are thinking about. Usually, you'll sleep a little better at night once your list is on paper.

Buy or Bring?

One of the most important decisions most expats make is whether to bring all their household goods with them, or to purchase new things here in Panama. Once you know what type of home or apartment you'll be living in – size, number of bedrooms, how much storage you'll have, etc. – you'll be in a better position to evaluate your options for your own situation. But let me make your consideration as simple as possible, based on what many expats have found.

I strongly recommend you ship as many of your physical belongings to Panama instead of buying them locally. Why? Because very little is manufactured in Panama, so furniture and household goods cost 25-30% more than you would pay for them in the U.S.

The range of selection you'll find locally is also limited. For example, a recent search in the city for a leather sectional couch yielded a mid-range brand name with a price tag of more than $5,000. A similar product in the States can be found for $1,600. While this is an extreme example, the reality is that many products are a limited commodity once they are shipped here, and retailers can charge exorbitant prices for them.

While a number of furniture stores exist in Panama City, the range of products and the quality of those products is generally much narrower than you will find in other countries. When we first came to Panama, we purchased a bedroom set with the bedframe and backboard, two bedside stands and a chest made out of composite wood structure. That purchase cost more than $6,500 in 2008. But alas, due to the high humidity and moving a number of times, the structure and materials literally came apart at the seams within the fourth year. Repair wasn't possible because of the wood composite material expanding from the humidity. (Note: When you can find solid wood to purchase locally, it's a better option, but it's also much more expensive. Once you've been here awhile, you can locate and hire local artisans to make solid wood furniture for you, which will be cheaper and last you a lifetime. Note: One does need to fumigate regularly in Panama due to the insect population, including termites.)

Things like towels, sheets, bedding or anything woven are also not manufactured in Panama. There's no Bed Bath & Beyond stores here, so plan in advance to bring these types of items with you when you move. If you choose to buy locally, plan to pay a whole lot more for the limited selection you will find. (Read more on local shopping resources in the next chapter.)

For those that prefer hard comparisons, keep the following two things in mind as part of your consideration:

- Quality and variety of the furniture or goods may vary greatly.
  - Shop around locally in Panama in advance of your move and get written quotes on what you find, including delivery and installation costs.
  - Compare what those purchases cost if bought in Panama, versus what you can buy (or bring) from home and ship.
- Get written shipping quotes, including door-to-door pick-up and delivery, from at least three reputable firms in your home country.
  - Many people are surprised when they realize that delivery *to their residence* in Panama on the shipped goods was not included in the original quote.
    - If it was not, this sometimes requires a separate hire locally from the contract you signed with your moving company at your pick-up in the States.
      - *Be sure you read the fine print to see that it's included.* Or you may have quite a hassle getting your things from the Customs office at the port in Panama to your actual residence, including additional fees and a customs broker, etc.
      - Additionally, be sure that installation and set-up is included on this end by the local firm.

○ Read the fine print about the insurance (and re-imbursement) coverage provided by your shipping company if any of your goods are broken or damaged during transit.

○ **Your container will be handled by many, many hands across the miles**. This is not as simple as a move from one state to another! A typical household international move of your things will likely include the following steps:

- Human hands to truck
- Truck to Container
- Container to Train
- Train to Truck
- Truck to Port
- Port to Crane
- Crane to Ship
- Ship to Crane
- Crane to Port
- Port to Truck
- Truck to Human hands

This last question is also very important because the last step listed here – truck to human hands – including getting your stuff off the truck, down or up the stairs, onto an elevator, through hallways and doorways to the state of being usable (or set up). This step alone is a very long process. Any breakage or damage to your goods is as likely to occur during this step as in any other. This is also due to the fact that the laborers who actually move your things locally are very likely *not trained* in the fine art of moving goods. As a result, you'll likely observe a lot of banging around. I strongly recommend you consider purchasing extra insurance in lieu of these realities.

Moving with a Pet

VETS is the most popular veterinarian group in the country

For those of us that choose to live abroad, one of the most painful choices to make can be whether or not to bring your beloved four-legged family members with you.

We brought three furry friends with us when we moved to Panama. We have many friends that (for whatever reason) chose to leave their pets with friends or family in their home country. Sometimes the pets were too old to make the trip.

Sometimes the new living environment was determined not to be ideal for the pets. Often there's still someone back at home who wants the pets to live with them. Many factors can come into play.

For us, it simply wasn't an option to leave our furry family members behind. And, if that's the case for you, it's important to understand what moving your pets entails.

Hire A Carrier or Do it Yourself?

First, there are two choices – to manage your pet's move yourself or to hire a professional pet carrier.

Moving your pet yourself

Preparing to move your pet by yourself involves concentrated, almost full-time focus in the weeks prior to your actual move, if you are coming from the States. Most paperwork must be completed ***within 10 days*** prior to your departure. If you screw this up, your pet will not be able to go with you, so pay attention.

First, contact your airline and get a copy of their requirements for transporting your pet. Once you have those in hand, make a list of all the things you need to do in order to prepare. Most airlines require that all needed documentation is filled out, verified, apostilled in your home country, and stamped by the Panamanian Embassy before your pet can board the plane. (An *apostille* is the equivalent of an international notary. Check with the Secretary of State's office in your city or state capitol for more information.)

Here's a list of the needed steps for moving your own pets, just to give you an idea. (Note that this is **not** an exhaustive list – it's just an overview.)

- Locate and purchase the needed materials for transit for your pet according to your airline's requirements.
  - Appropriately sized kennel – check the actual flight you are taking and to confirm what size will fit that particular plane
  - Water and food bowls, which fit inside the kennel
  - Zip ties to secure the kennel door closed during the flight
- Take your pet to the vet for the health check-up and to get the needed paperwork required by the airlines for the trip.
  - Your vet must sign the U.S. Department of Health forms, as there are strict guidelines for the pre-trip exam.
  - Many vets do not have this paperwork easily locatable in their offices, because they don't do many of these types of check-ups on a regular basis. Call your vet ahead of time to confirm that they know the reason for your visit, so they can be prepared for your appointment.
  - Plan for two to three return visits to the vet within the three weeks prior to your departure, in case any additional vaccinations or follow-up exams are required.

- Take the transit paperwork signed by your vet to the U.S. Department of Agriculture office nearest you to get it reviewed and approved.
  - There's a Department of Agriculture form that must be completed and submitted to them (including copies of the vet paperwork) with an accompanying fee.
- Next, all of the afore-mentioned paperwork must be taken to the local Secretary of State office to get internationally verified (an apostille).
  - This international verification paperwork is called an *Apostille*, and there is a fee involved per page.
- Send all the originals (and sometimes copies are also needed – check the country and airline requirements!) to the closest Panamanian Embassy to get their review and approval.
  - A limited number of Panamanian embassies exist in the U.S. and Canada;
  - Find out what the closest one is where you live;
  - Verify that the one closest to you accepts and processes pet relocation paperwork; and
  - Ship the the paperwork to that one via overnight courier, remembering that time is of the essence.
  - This will require at least two follow-up phone calls on your part to the embassy to make sure they received it, it's in process, and then, that it's on its way back to you.

- o Do this step as *soon* as the prior steps are completed, but within the 10 days, or your paperwork will be void and you'll have to start all over.

- Make copies of everything so you have them for your records. And by that, I mean every single page.

- All **original** paperwork must be attached to the kennel, when you check your pet in for the flight. The airlines do not accept copies.

Does all of this seem intimidating? It is, believe me. Hiring a professional pet mover can save you about 90% of the steps listed above, and save you significant stress.

Hiring the Professionals
There are people for hire – professional pet carriers – that will bring your dog, cat, bird or other species (each carrier has their own list) to Panama for you. This can cost upwards of $2,500-$5,000 or more *per animal*, depending on where you are coming from.

Yes, it's pricey, but when you hire a professional that's been there, done that – you're buying their expertise and know – how, as well as your own peace of mind.

Most of these professionals can be found online. Once you find them, call them. Talk to them. Review their websites carefully. Ask every possible question you can think of about how they manage pets in transit. Ask for references. Check the references you receive. Go with your gut feeling on your interactions with the prospective firms. If you feel comfortable with the people you hire, it will put your mind at ease during the actual move. You are placing the life of your furry family member in their hands, after all.

As you can see, taking it upon yourself to manage your own pet's move is involved and complicated. For me, it became close to a full-time job in between the moving, packing, and preparing activities that were happening for our overall household in the 10-day period before we actually boarded the plane.

Note that this process will be *very difficult* for someone who is working full-time; in fact, it will likely be impossible!

The key to doing it yourself successfully is the timeliness of all the paperwork. Ten days may seem like a long time, but when you add up all the above steps, it's really not long at all.

If it were me...

So, depending on your situation when you move to Panama, you may wish to go the professional route and hire someone. Yes, it's expensive. But it's the solution that I recommend to professionals coming to Panama. However, if you're looking at retirement, and have time on your hands, perhaps you can manage the do-it-yourself route.

Our own experience of moving our three pets to Panama was harrowing mentally and emotionally, and extremely time consuming. And we even had help locally! Several expats who've moved their own pets to Panama in recent years have told me the same.

If we had to do it over again, we'd hire a professional.

Finding a Home (or two)...

An Embera Indian village on the Chagres River

In Panama, whether you choose to live in the city, a rural town, or a place on the beach, finding your new home will never be as simple as it was back home. Anywhere in North America, finding a new house, condo, townhome or apartment can be done by pulling up the internet, downloading a number of real estate apps on your smart phone, or calling just one real estate agent. With just one of those actions, you'd be well on your way.

You'll be able to do the same things in Panama – even before you visit. But, this will just barely begin the process. Indeed, that's where the similarities end.

Panama's Multiple Listing System

In Panama, the first real Multiple Listing Service (MLS) has only recently been introduced by ACOBIR, the licensed real estate broker association, in the city. While this is something we take for granted in other parts of the world, the MLS is in its early infancy in Panama. And, to be honest, the entire real estate brokerage community is not completely behind the new MLS yet.

But, happily, the new system is taking shape. (When we came house-hunting back in 2008, no such system existed in any way, shape, or form.) That said, the local MLS will take several more years to function here in the way it's designed to, which is to say it will provide standardized, consistent information about real estate listings to potential buyers.

For many years in Panama, there has not been a consistent, reliable system for real estate listings in the country. And, yes, a significant amount of *Juega Vivo* became the norm in the industry. (*Juega Vivo* is the local term for of taking advantage of someone. For more on *Juega Vivo*, refer to Chapter 6 of the first book in this series.)

In recent past, this meant that when you were looking for a place to live, you'd discover the exact same real estate listing on different websites…listed by different brokers… at varying prices.

Because there was such a real estate boom in this country from 2003 to 2010, it seems that everyone became a real estate broker (with and without licenses), and mayhem ensued…all to the buyer's detriment, of course. For unsuspecting Gringos, there was no way to make sense of the system at all (mostly because there was no system!), except to know that you were likely being taken advantage of, or paying a Gringo price (versus the lower one a local resident might pay).

Hiring a Real Estate Broker

You may still run across some less than transparent real estate practices in Panama, unless you work with a solid real estate broker who you've found on personal referral.

Now, if you're like many Gringos, you may come to Panama with your Wild West spirit and think you can get around the *Juega Vivo* practice without a broker. And, if so, I truly wish you the best. But, based on hundreds of other Gringos who've been there, done that, I can tell you that you'll likely end up exactly the same way as they have… feeling disillusioned, taken advantage of, disappointed, and having wasted significant time and money in the process. Don't take that chance.

Play it safe. Protect yourself in the largest investment you'll make here in your new country, and hire a *licensed* real estate broker. I delineate the word 'licensed' here because it's important. Some brokers you will find online are not registered with the government, and while they can help you, they can't legally sign the paperwork with you.

It's for your own protection to ask the question *'Are you licensed?'* before you start working with someone, so that you don't end up in any questionable situations involving your money or your new abode down the road.

When you require your broker to be licensed, you are contributing to the positive evolution of the Panama real estate community.

A broker can only be licensed through Panama's Ministry of Commerce and Industry, which requires them to agree to a set of ethical practices. These ethical practices are similar to what you're used to when you conduct business with a real estate professional in the U.S. or in most other developed nations. They are for your protection.

Six questions to ask before you hire a broker

Here's a list of questions which may seem obvious if you are looking for real estate in other markets, but you can't assume are standard in the Panama market. Take note of these to ensure you're hiring a person you can trust to represent your interests with integrity and transparency.

1. Are you (personally) a licensed real estate broker in the Republic of Panama? If not, who in your firm holds the actual brokerage license?
2. Can you personally sign purchase or sale contracts? If not, who within your brokerage signs those?
3. Can you provide a translation of the sales contract into English (assuming you, as the buyer, do not speak Spanish) for me to review in advance of any contract needing to be signed?
4. Are you open to working with other brokers in locating a place that's right for me/my family? If so, how will that process work?
5. What brokerage commission will you be paid once a home purchase (or rental) is located and agreed upon?
6. If the home we select is represented by a different broker, what will that broker be paid as commission?

Get ready to be patient

Once you find a broker you trust and feel comfortable with, take the time to let them find you the place that will work best for you. Because your broker is having to navigate a system that is not easy to maneuver, it's important to realize that this process will take *much longer* than you might hope, even for an established professional in the local market.

The complaint I hear most frequently from local brokers about their clients from abroad is this: the clients get upset when things don't happen rapidly.

News flash, future clients! Things in Panama don't happen rapidly. Adjust your expectations. Allow your broker the same benefit that you will find you have with your own processes in Panama – things are going to take much, much longer than you'd hoped. So, be patient with your broker, knowing that they have to navigate a difficult system.

In order to manage your own expectations when it comes to a real estate transaction, be sure to ask your broker what you should expect in terms of a *reasonable* timeline.

Get your questions answered before you sign

The ideal scenario would be if the real estate firm you choose provides a list of Frequently Asked Questions for buyers new to Panama. What a great idea! But even if they don't, have all these above conversations *before* you start the process of looking for a new home. When you know this information upfront, you'll find yourself less frustrated and feeling more in control of the process. (Yes, it will still be a roller coaster and likely maddening, but less so.)

Expat Owned (and trusted) Real Estate Firms in Panama
I have numerous recommendations from many, many buyers who have used the following three firms. Every report I have heard about these three has been that they found their dealings with them to be extremely professional and ethical. I've also personally met the owners and several brokers from all three of the following firms, and have been impressed with each.

None of these firms are aware I am listing their firms in this book. So, while each of these is owned and managed by an expat from the U.S., it's *still recommended* that you contact each one, meet with each one, and get a gut feel for the one that best fits your needs.

Certainly, there will be other firms in country that you may discover, or that have been recommended to you by others that will fit the bill for your needs. However, my goal here is to share those resources that have turned into good experiences for myself and others.

Inside Panama Real Estate
Based in Panama (city), Coronado (beaches), and Boquete (Interior)
www.insidepanamarealestate.com

Panama Equity
Based in Panama (city) but covers the entire country
www.panamaequity.com

Re/Max Beaches & City
Based in the Coronado beach area but cover the entire country
www.beachesandcity.com

The bottom line on choosing a broker to meet your needs is to conduct your own due diligence, check references carefully, and meet with them to ensure their personality and work style works for *you*.

Finding your new home, whether you purchase or rent, is a decision that will have the greatest impact on your lifestyle in your new country. Your new home becomes your refuge in the storm, so to speak, for your new life. Take this process seriously and allow more time than you think you'll need to locate the property that you're really looking for.

Things to Keep in Mind when You're Shopping for Real Estate in Panama

When we rented our first apartment in Panama, we found a number of aspects from that process to be surprising, based on our experiences back home.

Here are a few things to keep in mind when you're buying (or renting) in the Panama real estate market.

This list will help you with your budget planning in your real estate decisions.

- It's your responsibility to confirm that the ownership title of your new unit is free and clear (and able to be transferred to you) with the government before you sign final purchase or lease agreements.
  - o Any real estate broker worth his salt knows this, and will walk you through how the process is to be done.
  - o This confirmation is not a given, but it's for your protection to demand that it be done as a prerequisite to your deal getting finalized.
  - o Ask for a copy of this confirmation document from the government before you arrive at the meeting where you'll be expected to sign any final real estate transfer, lease or mortgage documents.

- Most homes or apartments are sold or leased to their new occupants *without* appliances. This means that the stove, oven, refrigerator, washer/dryer, air conditioning wall units, and the like may be visible when you view the property (if it is still occupied) but are not included in the purchase price and may be ripped out before you take possession.
  - o Be sure to clarify this with your real estate broker.
  - o Some properties do include these items, but if so, it's a higher price.

- Most properties *do not include* screens on the windows. Yes, this is surprising in a climate where all kinds of critters fly. (Refer to other types of tropical adjustments in Chapter 8.)

- Window coverings, curtains and light fixtures are generally not included in the purchase price of your unit. (This means you will have to buy your own.)
- The ugly in-wall air conditioning units you will see in most properties in Panama are called *splits*.
  - o Splits are less efficient, and they are also a completely different cooling experience than Central A/C. These are the norm in Panama.
  - o If you find a unit with Central A/C, you will likely pay a higher price.
- Most stovetops in Panama are gas operated, which is good because it means you can still cook (if/and) when the electricity goes out.
- The cost of electricity in Panama is three times the cost of most places in the U.S.
  - o Keep in mind, however, that the monthly bill will depend on how much you run the A/C in your unit. I can tell you it was a *big* shock when our first month's bill arrived with a $800 balance.

The Affordability of Weekend Retreat Homes

Many expats find that because real estate pricing in the country is less expensive than where they came from that their budget allows them the luxury of buying or renting a weekend home, away from the city.

If you elect to become a city dweller, you may – like many locals – find you enjoy spending weekends and holidays in the country's Interior. (The Interior is anything located West of the Arraijan and Chorrera suburbs outside the city of Panama.) If that's the case, then you'll be able to find lots of real estate options to suit your taste.

Condo and home rentals on or close to the Pacific coast beaches are plentiful. One of my real estate friends told me a couple of years ago that there were close to 40 real estate developments started or under construction on the Pacific coast. I'm not aware of what this number is today. So, there are plenty of existing homes and condos to choose from, as well as lots of new inventory offered in pre-sales at the present time.

For those preferring a slightly cooler climate, check out Boquete (which you already read about in Chapter 3), Volcan Baru, El Valle, or Cerro Azul. (Cerro Azul is not in the Interior – it's actually East of the city, about an hour out of town, but enjoys a cooler climate because of it's topography.) Each of these *pueblos* vary in distance from the city and offer a range of rustic to newly built homes. Condominiums are not as plentiful as they are in the city in the rural towns, but some do exist.

One of the highlights of my time in Panama was relishing the peace and quiet at our weekend home on the Pacific coast. In addition to getting away from the chaos of the city, the easy access to the beach gave us a place to disconnect entirely from the rest of the world. We enjoyed being able to afford this luxury as part of our Panama experience.

Please note that in all of this talk about real estate, you see that I never said real estate in Panama is cheap. I don't believe it is. However, you may find – like many other expats – that real estate is more affordable in the country than it is in other places. Obviously, your perspective on this will vary, depending on if you're from Omaha or New York City.

13
PLUGGING INTO LOCAL LIFE

ONE OF THE most common complaints in Panama from new expats is that they don't know how to find things that they're looking for. It's true that this can be a challenge.

Using the Yellow Pages is pretty tough if you have little to no Spanish skills. The same goes for the Yellow Pages website, www.paginasamarillas.com. Signage in Panama is for the most part also in Spanish, as well. And even if you can read most signs, you'll see that the signage system is not always laid out in a way that makes sense to the Westerner brain.

Indeed, the whole system of finding information in Panama is wholly different from anywhere else I've ever seen, and in truth, it's almost a comedy of errors in calling it a *'system'* because there really isn't one. Most expats – even Spanish speaking ones – get pretty darn frustrated in the first few months living here, because the places they'd expect to find listings or portals of information simply don't exist. Not yet.

The best rule of thumb for finding what you're looking for is to ask for help – from your new expat friends, from your building administration, and from anyone else who has lived in-country for a while. These referrals are always your best resource. With time, your own experiences will add up to referrals you can share with other new expats.

What follows in this chapter is intended to give you a leg up on finding a few things – a good restaurant, a place to keep fit, news resources in English, a place to donate your clothes, and places to shop. It was in my own search for finding these kinds of things that I really began to appreciate how necessary my Spanish skills were, in those early years of living here.

Finding a Good Restaurant

*A **típico** meal of fried corvina and patacones*

One of the distinct beauties of Panama is that you can find good food from all over the world right here in the city. Because ships traverse the Canal every day from every point of the globe and those ships bring (and have brought) people from all over the world here, it's safe to assume that this is how many people originally found their way to this country. (The Canal is not the only reason people come to Panama, but as the isthmus's largest economic generator, it's safe to attribute a large percentage of population growth to it.)

Today, the international fare that can be enjoyed in Panama reflects this global crossroads mentality. Yes, you can find the local standards like warm, baked empanadas with cheese, pork or *carne* (beef) and *patacones* (fried plantains). Comfort can be found in a cup of the local chicken soup, *sancocho*, on almost every street corner. Most new expats are intrigued by all the exotic fruits at the grocery store. But, this is just the beginning.

Dining out in Panama is not just about food, however. Dining out here is also a social affair. The North American habit of turning tables – two, three or four times – within an evening does not exist in Panama to many a Gringo's delight. In fact, most of the time, it's culturally assumed that when you eat out in Panama, you'll stay at your table for as long as you like.

Interestingly enough, the practice of the restaurant al-lowing you to linger over your meal is so common that you may have a hard time getting your server to bring you the check when you're ready for it. It seems the local wait staff habitually disappears, the moment you've had your apertifs and your *postre* (dessert). You will often find that you have to track the server down just to get the bill. Then, you'll have to track him down again once when you are ready to pay! What a difference this is from the dining scene in North America, where you're literally rushed through a meal with the check shoved under your nose before you've taken the last bite. I love the fact that eating out in Panama is a leisurely pursuit.

In Chapter 7, in the section titled *Getting Off the Beaten Path*, I reference *DeGusta Panama*. This is a website and an app that can help you find a number of places that will tickle your culinary fancy here in Panama, (though it is in Spanish). Below I've listed some of the restaurants I enjoyed the most during my time in Panama.

Market in Bella Vista

Entrepreneur David Hennessy owns and operates some of Panama's best restaurants. This is one of them. With an open, airy feel, Market is one of the top places for a business (or leisure) lunch. Market reminds me of New York with its white-covered tables and waiters sporting slick-backed hair. This is a good, dependable standard for lunch or dinner, with a varied menu of salads, sandwiches, USDA steaks, fresh fish and many other options.

La Posta in Bella Vista

Another of Hennessy's restaurants, La Posta feels like the Latin restaurants I've seen in movies depicting a Cuban flair. The décor is refined tropical. Ceiling fans turn lazily above you. The wait staff wear clean, white aprons, and are pleasant and attentive. Here, expect to find excellent continental fare with wonderful fish selections and interesting desserts. La Posta is our family's hands-down favorite for visiting out-of-town guests.

Burger place atop Manrey Hotel, Bella Vista

(Naturally, I could not find the name of this place on their website...go figure!)

I know. You did not come to Panama to eat burgers. But believe me, after a month of living here and eating fish almost daily, you'll be jones-ing for a good burger. When you reach that point, this is the place to come. The restaurant is on the rooftop inside the Manrey Hotel. Order outside while lounging around the pool or having cocktails and enjoying the view of the city. Any type of burger you can think of, they make, and they make them well.

Gaucho's Steakhouse, Bella Vista

Gaucho's is a true Argentinian steak house. They do meat well, and they do it right. Sit down to red and white checkered tablecloths, large cuts of beef, and delicious desserts. Martini drinkers, you'll feel right at home here. Don't come here for the fish; steak is what they do. Gaucho's is very popular with traveling business people.

Cholo's, Pacific coast beach area, Coronado

Cholo's is hard to find in Coronado. It used to be right on the Pan-American Highway. Then, the owner packed up, moved across the highway and down a side street. There's no sign on the highway to indicate where to turn, which can be confusing. Open for breakfast, lunch and dinner on certain days (and this changes all the time), this place offers simple Mexican fare with ample portions. The owner is a lovely Mexican woman who has lived in Panama for many years, and uses many of her grandfather's authentic recipes. While service is erratic at times, Cholo's is very popular with expats. We love Cholo's for a late lunch after a morning at the beach. Make note that it's usually packed on the weekends.

Manolo Carocol, Casco Viejo

This is a fantastic Spanish restaurant serving tapas and amazing wines for dinner. One of the first places at which we dined after coming to Panama…this place is truly a pleasurable eating *experience*. There's no set menu. You simply make a reservation, show up and they tell you when you are seated what the evening's fares will be. Then, they serve you over, and over, and over again. Expect to depart feeling stuffed and happy. Highly recommended for any occasion that calls for fine dining. You'll always need a reservation.

Balboa Yacht Club, Amador Causeway

The BYC is located a block from TGI Friday's and the Country Inn and Suites (facing the Canal and the Bridge of the Americas)

The BYC is an open air, casual restaurant overlooking the mouth of the Panama Canal. Wood tables and chairs with umbrellas are a great place to enjoy a burger, fish sandwich, and a beer and catch a nice breeze. This is a great place to hang out with friends and relax. Occasionally, the BYC hosts local bands, if you're up to sticking around for some live music and a spin around the dance floor as the night wears on. You'll hear a lot of English spoken here. One of our favorite hangouts for the past few years, many liken this popular expat watering hole to Cheer's, where if you come often enough, everyone knows your name.

Hungry for Breakfast?

There are places you can go in Panama for a tasty brunch, if you like buffets. But, I'm one of those people who doesn't appreciate others looking at my food, much less sneezing on it as they review the options, so I tend to skip the buffet places.

One of the things I miss the most about the U.S. is going out for brunch on Sunday morning. Typical breakfast food in Panama is very different than what you'll find in North America. Me? I like eggs, hash browns, toast, coffee, and occasionally, eggs benedict or a short stack of pancakes.

In Panama, you'll find a lot more meat on the menu for breakfast and fewer sweets, unless you're staying in a hotel. Roadside stands sell warm empanadas for breakfast with pork, beef or cheese inside for on-the-go eaters. A sit-down Panamanian breakfast includes eggs, a cube steak mix called *Steak Picato* made up of sautéed onions and tomatoes, and thick, deep-fried corn tortillas. Locals love some type of meat with every type of meal, and that includes breakfast.

For those that prefer the North American type of breakfast, unless you go to a big hotel, your standard IHOP menu selection is in short order locally. Crepes & Waffles is the next best thing.

Best brunch place on a lazy weekend day:
Crepes & Waffles, Bella Vista

The strange thing about Crepes & Waffles is that while a good part of their menu offers breakfast items, they're not actually open until Noon. This seems like heresy to me. But you have to get used to it if you want to enjoy their food.

There are a number of Crepes & Waffles locations around the city. We prefer the one in Bella Vista. The restaurant is clean, the décor is simple, and the food is relatively consistent. On offer: Eggs, omelets, waffles, crepes, coffee, fruit, *batidos* (shakes), and the like. Everything comes a la carte, so order exactly what you want – there are no sides here.

Best "Greasy Spoon" breakfast:
Hotel Ejecutivo (Executive Hotel)

I'd lived in Panama for six years before I finally ate here. Once I did, I berated myself for waiting that long! The breakfasts here are just like ones I used to eat with my dad when I was in high school at the local diner where I grew up in the South: cheese omelets, black coffee and a stack of simple pancakes. Just like I like 'em. Unfortunately, they don't serve cheese grits.

Hidden in the banking district, the décor of this hotel restaurant is a throwback to the 1980's: all beige and mauve and wintergreen. Valet parking is available on the days they offer it (hey, it's Panama) at the front door of the hotel. Prepare to wait on the weekends if you don't arrive before 11, as this is a popular place with locals.

The World is Your Oyster

The best news about Panama's dining scene is that this short list is just the beginning. From roadside patio seating to white table-clothed dining, Panama has new restaurants opening all the time. Between the time I write this and when it's published, there'll be ten new places open and operating. That means you'll always have plenty of options for your dining pleasure. That's one of the things I enjoy most about Panama: good food and plenty of choices.

Buen provecho! When your meal arrives, it's considered good manners in Panama to salute your tablemates with this phrase before you dig in. (It's the Spanish equivalent for Good Eating! Or Bon Appetit!)

Panama's Favorite Casinos

For those of you that like to roll the dice, Panama very likely has a casino that would love to take your money. It is important to note, however, that Panama is definitely not Las Vegas. Yes, gambling is completely legal here, but there's only a handful casinos in the city. For those accustomed to the sheen and shine of big city casinos, that means there are probably only a short list of places here you might really want to visit.

I'm not personally a big gambler, so I asked fellow expats to fill in the gaps for me on this particular topic about their personal experiences and recommendations on their favorite gaming locales.

The Veneto

The best-known casino in the city is within the Veneto Hotel in Panama's El Cangrejo neighborhood downtown. This casino has been around quite some time on Panama's gambling scene, and features 40,000 square feet of space to roll whatever type of game you're up to. The Veneto's website claims they have 15 poker tables, 40 other types of game tables and 600 slots. Whatever your gambling pleasure, the casino operates 24/7 and offers blackjack, poker, baccarat, craps, and roulette. There's also a private VIP room for the big spenders.

Expat Skyler Ralston was a frequent poker player at the Veneto in prior years, spending two to three nights a week on the local circuit. She enjoyed playing at the Veneto because the ambience there is "full of energy at the tables games, and full of concentration at the poker tables." (She also claims she fooled, bluffed and raked in her opponent's money on a regular basis, because her ability was often assumed to be "clueless" since she's a young, blonde Gringa. Could this be an example of the prevalent female stereotypes that still exist in Latin America? Hmm… Read Skyler's Panama story in Chapter 11.)

Drinks are free when you're playing the tables, but be forewarned that the ladies of the night do populate this establishment with regularity. Prostitution is legal in Panama, and this is one of the well-known pick-up points for the trade (as are many other nightlife venues).

Other Large Casino Brands

Here's a short list of other popular larger casinos in the city, populated from memory and a little help from website TripAdvisor.com:

- Hotel El Panama
- Hotel Riande
- Continental Hotel
- Marriott Hotel
- The Majestic Casino
- The Casino at the Panama Hilton

Note that this is only a list and not a recommendation. I've never even set foot in any of these personally, except to walk past their entryways.

Smaller, Local Casinos

Canadian expat David Arias chimed in on Google+ and said he enjoys the Golden Lion Casino in El Dorado, calling it "quiet, clean and nicely designed." He also noted that the $0.25 wings served on Mondays, Wednesdays and Sundays are also "a good size and delicious." (Who can argue with a great price and tasty snacks?)

U.S. expat Randy Hilarski (www.randyhilarski.com) reports that his favorite casino is more popular with the locals than tourists (which makes sense, as I'd never heard of this one until he mentioned it): Bingo 90. Located in Obarrio, Randy said the "food is decent, there's no loud music, and they have plenty of servers waiting to help." (Note that this particular casino does not offer table games, however.)

Finding Local News in English

Most of the media resources you'll find in Panama are in Spanish, so many expats with limited or no Spanish language skills have a hard time even locating the basics. Following are some English language resources that will be of help to you, as you get settled here.

Panama Expat Print Newspaper

The Visitor is a weekly newspaper printed by some expats who've been in Panama for a long time. It's 24-36 pages, more or less, and in it, you'll find stories of interest about life in Panama, ongoing events and a lot of businesses advertising to English speakers. It's currently the only local

English newspaper available countrywide. The Visitor also has a website at www.TheVisitorPanama.com.

Online local website for daily Panama news
The Panama Guide at www.Panama-Guide.com is a locally produced website in English with updated daily news. It's the most comprehensive website you'll find with all the latest news happening in the country. You can sign up for email updates there, though there is a small fee to be on their mailing list. There are hundreds of articles from recent months, so if you're seeking any historical data in a certain recent time period, this is the most convenient place to find it.

Morning radio show in English
The Breakfast Show is a locally-produced radio program in English on FM Radio 89.3 The emcee is a British resident named Gerry D. The format of the show is a typical drive-time one from 7 AM to 10 AM that features music, interviews and local news. You can also tune in online at www.PBCPanama.com and listen in from wherever you are in the world.

Panama Craig's List Equivalent
www.Encuentra24.com – This online resource is mostly in Spanish, and it's the Latin American equivalent to Craig's List. Here you'll find local listings for real estate, products for sale, services and the like. There are some listings in English, but you have to sort through to find them. This can be a

good practice for your burgeoning language skills, but it's helpful to keep a dictionary close by, if so. Or, you can use the Google Translate app to help.

Panama Tourism Website in English

PanamaInfo.com – This is the main tourism website for the country in English. There are some good general resources here, but most of it is geared toward visitors, not new residents.

Beauty Services

If you're already read my first book in the Gringo Guide to Panama series, then you know that services in Panama, as a whole, are pretty affordable. That includes services that we women enjoy, like manicures, pedicures, massage, haircuts and color. Panama also offers plenty of places for facials, micro-derm abrasion and other such necessary services for those who seek to turn back the clock.

When you're new to Panama, you'll notice little signs here and there in salon windows that read "Blower – $5". You can probably imagine the word I kept thinking of every time I saw these signs when we first moved to town, and they always made me laugh.

But no, the signs aren't advertising a type of sexual favor. They're talking about blowing out your hair with a hair dryer. In the U.S., we refer to that same service as a *style*.

In Latin America, it's a common practice to go to the salon with wet hair and have a professional blow dry and style it for you – before you go to work, to dinner, or a special event.

But you get the picture. In Panama, you'll generally find this service for $5-$10.

Finding the Salon that works for you

So, where's a girl to go for a good haircut, style, color, straightening or a wax? Here in Panama, beauty salons abound on almost every street corner, as Latin women love to feel pretty and they commit a large percentage of their time and income to doing just that. (Of course, when you only pay the nominal prices for beauty services available in Panama, there's no reason *not* to go, in my opinion.)

Just like anywhere else in the world, you might have to kiss a few frogs before you find the salon or beauty shop that's right for you. Ladies, you can expect to pay as little as $12 for a manicure and $20 for a haircut in Panama. Higher-end salons charge much more – $35 and up for a ladies cut, and $65 and up for color, depending on if you want all over color or highlights (or both).

There are a few salons that taut their talent with foreign types of hair. When you go there, you can expect to pay more. The upside is that they are more adept – generally – at Gringo hair, which is a commodity here.

The typical type of hair on a local's head may be very different from yours in terms of texture, thickness, curl, etc. The best rule of thumb for finding a salon professional that fits your needs is to ask the other Gringos who live here. When you like someone else's do, ask them for a referral.

Waxing Genius

One beauty service that's even more common than cuts and color is hair removal. By that I mean, waxing. Most every salon in the country does waxing of all sorts, including the famous Brazilian bikini wax. (For those of you unfamiliar with the Brazilian, it means all the hair in the bikini area is removed.) Because our Latin and black sisters often have heavier body hair than those with lighter color skin, waxing is big business in Panama.

Many of the salons I've visited over the years have Colombian professionals doing the waxing, and they're quite adept at it, for whatever reason. The good news is that wherever you don't want hair, you can get it ripped out really cheap almost everywhere you go in Panama. A number of wax-only salons also exist. I recommend Professional Body Waxing, which has three or four locations in Panama City.

Beauty salons are required to be licensed here in the country, but that really just means the individuals working there attended some kind of training. Normally, it does not guarantee that the salon's hygiene will be up to the standards you'd expect, nor that the service you receive will be as sophisticated as you've experienced back home.

I recommend visiting a salon before you make an appointment for a service to check it out for yourself. Talk to the owner or manager, observe the clients departing (after their service is complete), check out their professional tools and make sure to visit the bathroom. (The bathroom's cleanliness will tell you a lot.)

Salons that Specialize in Expat Hair

Here's a couple of salons that many of my expat friends frequent here in the city. *(NOTE: Each of these salons charges more than the prices I've noted in the paragraphs above. It's best to ask what the expected price will be before you commit, so that you aren't surprised.)*

Moonlight Studio on Avenida Balboa off the Cinta Costera: Under new ownership recently. Phone: 391-0842 or email info@moonlightbeautystudio.com

Talking Heads Studio in Clayton (City of Knowledge) – Paula, the very friendly owner from the U.K., did my hair for several years and did a good job. She has a loyal following. Phone: 317-1091 or 317-1092

Saloon Hair Wellness Panama (The Village Mall, Coronado): Aldo de Martino from Italy moved to Panama in 2013, and married his Panamanian sweetheart. Vincent opened his shop in late 2014, and hands-down, gave me the best haircuts I ever had in country. He's an expert with short hair. 344-7891, +507-6500-8761

For the Picky amongst us

At the end of the day, you – like me – may find that you just can't find someone who consistently gives you the cut and style you really like in the Panama market.

This is not uncommon for Gringos.

For years, the only remedy that worked for me was to have my hair done back in the States when we visited, and then get touch ups and trims in Panama. We were fortunate to go back and forth every four months or so, so this worked for me.

However, even if you prefer to have your hair done back home, you may wish to get introduced to a stylist here in Panama, in case you want a special up-do or style prior to an event. I recommend trying a few local resources to have in your back pocket for that purpose. Plus, you might just find a stylist that does what you need for a very low price.

Keeping Fit

These days, it seems everyone is crazy about being in shape. The fitness craze wasn't all that big a deal when we first came to Panama in early 2008. But then in 2012 or so, something happened, and fitness became all the rage.

It seems these days that everyone is fixated on some hyper-level of fitness – whether it's training at the gym, running, biking, hiking, or a class activity like yoga or pilates. For expats new to Panama, one of the first things you often look for is....somewhere to take the edge off the move, right? So, what are some expat-friendly options for working out in in the city?

Health Clubs

The most popular chain of health clubs is PowerCLUB. According to their website, they now have 12 locations in Panama City. (When we first arrived, it was only five, so they've grown.) Depending on which club you visit, you'll find a fully-equipped gym with free weights, weight machines, ellipticals, a full roster of classes, and in some cases, racquet ball courts. The newest location in Panama Pacifico even has a refurbished Olympic-size outdoor pool and a separate pool for the kids.

Other smaller health clubs are available in certain neighborhoods, but PowerCLUB is the biggest and best. They also offer an All-Club membership, so you can visit whichever location you want.

Yoga and Pilates

A number of studios for both yoga and pilates have sprung up since 2008. I'm a yoga fanatic, so I sought out as many as I could find when we first arrived. At that time, there were only three, and the types of yoga they taught could only be described as basic, hatha yoga. Not for me. In 2016, there's a dozen full-on yoga studios with professionally trained teachers and classes. Most of them are still focused on morning or evening time slots to suit the working crowd. Classes range in cost, so check the studio's Facebook page or website for specifics.

Pilates did not exist in Panama in 2008; the first studios began opening up in mid 2010. Now in early 2016, there are listings for about a dozen studios in and around the city, possibly more. I went to one in Albrook for about a year until it closed, and have not been to any others, but I see the signs and ads for them around the city. There's also a couple of gals who teach Pilates in their homes (or their outdoor patio spaces) who were trained in the U.S. in the Clayton area. So, good news, options abound for those crazy about pilates. Most of what I've seen in Panama is reformer pilates – the kind that uses the machines. Classes for mat pilates may exist; I just have not seen those widely advertised to date.

Running, Jogging, and Biking Outdoors

Panama's Cinta Costera along the Panama Bay

If you're a runner, you have a choice of three big park areas in the city. The first is the Cinta Costera, which is the main artery through town along the Panama Bay waterfront. It's long and pretty, but you're running right alongside all the traffic, which is noisy and smells like exhaust at peak traffic times. At low tide, the east end of the Cinta also smells badly of sewage, which is pretty unpleasant. (Note that this will be fixed in the coming years when the new Bay clean-up and wastewater treatment plants are completed, but that's still a few years out.)

The second large park in the city is Parque Omar, which is the largest park located in the San Francisco neighborhood. High-end homes and condominiums surround this park, and if you choose to live in one of them, you can literally walk out your back door and enter the park. Parque Omar has lovely walking paths, good security and plenty of parking. On the weekends, local events are often hosted here, and a number of farmer's market vendors offer their fresh wares to the public. The park also has a large public library.

Your third option for outdoor space is the Amador Causeway, which is on the west edge of the city. This area is my favorite because it offers more than six miles of safe pathways and roads, along the Panama Canal. The views here are spectacular too. A few vendors offering bike and motorcycle rental are located here, as well as multiple restaurants and tourist shops.

For those that work or live in Panama Pacifico – the redevelopment of the former U.S. Air Force base on the west side of the city – miles of wide streets and sidewalks abound. So much so, that the community hosts road races and outdoor activities on a regular basis for a number of clubs.

For trail running, you'll find a couple of very active clubs in the city for this purpose. ASICS has one they support, and they do a number of foot races during the year. Their website identifies a number of races the group hosts each year which are open to the public.

So, new expats, the good news is…you have options for staying fit in Panama. (This assumes, of course, that acclimating and sweating in the tropical humidity is not enough.) If you're not keen on profuse sweating, then just walking down the street may be enough for you. In fact, most expats tend to experience mild weight loss without exercise after they've been in Panama for several months, due to dietary changes (more fish) and the climate. That's as long as you don't make *patacones* (fried plantains) a regular staple in your weekly diet, anyway.

Shopping Destinations

Albrook Mall

Panama has become a shopping destination for visitors from Central and South America in recent years. Many people come to the city and the Colon Free Trade Zone from other countries solely to take advantage of lower prices and more availability of products, than what they can find in their home countries. The country now markets itself in Latin America as a shopping destination.

Malls in the city

The city of Panama is fortunate to have a number of malls. Generally, the stores you will find yourself frequenting on a regular basis will be located inside one of these shopping centers.

The habit of cruising the mall is very much a cultural trend in Panama. (Cruising the mall is what my parents called it; younger generations call it hanging out at the mall.) But it's not just tourists and teenagers that frequent these halls of shopping. Here, you'll see every member of the family in attendance, from grandparents to infants. Going to the mall in Panama is truly a social affair, and for many working class families – it's also a place to stay cool in the air conditioning on the weekends. (Take a look at this when you visit the malls locally – you can tell the difference between who's actually shopping and who's just hanging out by those carrying bags of purchased items.)

Here's a brief description of each mall in the city.

Multiplaza Mall

Known as the most upscale mall in the city until Soho debuted last year, Multiplaza is across the street from the Punta Pacifica Hospital, and located in the trendy, high-rise neighborhood that bears the same name (Punta Pacifica). Here you can shop in Louis Vuitton, Givenchy, Tiffany, Kenneth Cole or Cartier, with the added convenience of valet parking if you choose. You'll also find a number of brands from Europe and South America that you may not be familiar with – Zara, Velez, Whoops, Estampa, and MNG, among others.

Multiplaza is also a good place to find some tasty casual restaurants in the city. Which is good news, because it means you won't go hungry as you're making the rounds. (Going to the mall for me always means some kind of fun eating too.)

Insider tip: Have lunch at Tomate, which is located in the middle of a hallway on the bottom floor near one of the escalators. Tomate offers fresh salads, sandwiches and smoothies, which are healthy and tasty. (Tomate also has a location at Albrook Mall.)

A couple of other locales worth mentioning that you normally don't find in a mall, but you will find at Multiplaza: Riba Smith supermarket (Panama's most affluent grocery store), Do It Center and Novey (the two local hardware chains), furniture stores, and Mosaic Spa.

A new wing was added to Multiplaza in December 2012. This newer area features a large Felix Maduro department store, and some of the U.S. brands like Banana Republic, Bebe and Victoria's Secret. (You'll notice that V Secret does not sell underwear in Panama – just its perfume and body care lines.)

Multicentro

One of the original malls in Panama, Multicentro is a middle-class offering in the city. Connected to the Hard Rock Hotel by a walkway, and across the street from the Decapolis Radisson Hotel, Multicentro also includes it's own casino inside.

Some of the better-known stores you'll find in Multicentro include Hilfiger, Hilfiger Denim, Lacoste, Guess, Nautica, Clark's, and Nike, among many other local and Latin American brands.

Multicentro also has a real estate brokerage, a Kosher supermarket (in the basement) and Panama's Conway store, which is the closest thing you'll find to a Target in the country. Families love the bowling alley, cinema and entertainment zone on the top floor.

Albrook Mall

Albrook Mall sits adjacent to the Marcos A. Gelabert International Airport, in the neighborhood of the same name (Albrook). Albrook was part of the old American Canal Zone.

The colorful façade of this particular shopping center is eye-catching, if not a little garish, but I actually think it's kind of fun. The mall is adjacent to the Municipal Transportation Terminal, which is a hub for all the national and local bus routes. This is convenient if you're on your way in or out of town. A new Aloft hotel with a direct entrance to the mall is now open.

In Albrook, every wing within the mall is identified by the use of an animal icon. You'll see signs indicating that you are in the giraffe, rhinoceros or bear sections, which helps when you're trying to locate yourself and your car. Mall security personnel are attired like zookeepers, which is an added point of interest. A huge food court offers everything you can possibly imagine from coffee to ice cream to Wendy's. Children of all ages love the full-size merry-go-round.

Albrook Mall has come a long way in the past two years after undergoing a big facelift including a new higher-end wing added in 2012. The new wing includes Gap, Banana Republic, Bebe, Clark's, Adidas and many others. This mall also includes a two-level Arrocha, which is Panama's best-known chain of drug store (akin to a Walgreens or Boots). This mall is so big, you could spend the entire day there, and buy everything from furniture to clothes and shoes, see a doctor, get your groceries, do a bit of gambling, bowl, eat, and then return to your house on the local bus.

It's best to wear your most comfortable walking shoes for the Albrook experience.

Metro Mall
Opened in 2011, this is the closest mall to Tocumen International Airport. While I haven't been there personally, I'm told it's similar to Multiplaza and Albrook, though not quite as large. Since it is closest to the airport, many tourists come in for a day or two of shopping and take buses directly there.

SOHO
Panama's luxury destination for shopping in the city is located on Calle 50 inside a stunning high-rise hotel and office tower that just opened in 2015. Reminiscent of its namesake, this shopping mecca is fast becoming known for the crème de la crème of shopping in Panama. The atmosphere is absolutely gorgeous inside and boasts top-notch brands like Burberry, Chanel, Calvin Klein, Dior, Fendi, Hackett, Kate Spade and Jimmy Choo. Have a cappuccino or high tea at one of the sit-down restaurants inside or catch the latest thriller at Panama's newest cinema. But don't be intimidated all the gloss, the glass and the visible security. In late December 2015, I found cheaper prices here than I did at Multiplaza on some clothing items and electronics. While it's not as big – yet – as Multiplaza, Soho is definitely worth a visit just to take it all in.

Westlands

Westlands Mall is located in the District of Arraijan, the large suburb west of the city. The newest mall in and around the city that opened in late 2012, Westlands features a cinema, grocery store, a large Arrocha, and many other stores. Because of its location, it's a natural place to stop on your way from the city to the Pacific coast beaches.

Residents of the communities of Arraijan and Chorrera, which include more than 300,000 citizens, were glad to finally get their own mall when Westlands opened in 2012. This mall is worth a visit for convenience alone if you live West of the Panama Canal.

Buying Apparel Locally

As you can see, there's lots of shopping choices in Panama. Not included here are plenty of other *locales* in stand-alone locations or strip malls all over the city. The malls are the most orderly experience you'll find in the country, which is why they're the most obvious choice for most expats.

While Panama tauts itself for shopping for tourists from Latin America, it is not necessarily the least expensive choice for you, if you come from North America. We personally never did much of our shopping in Panama for clothing and shoes. Some of this had to do with taste.

The local wares of the better-known U.S. and European brands in this market are targeted to Latin American consumers. For women's shoes, for example, this may mean that the color palette is very colorful and in most cases, very eye-catching. While flats have only recently become readily available in Panama, the choices you'll encounter in local stores are very, very different from what you'll find up North.

Certainly in women's clothing, the norm in the local market wares is much more colorful, revealing and adventurous than you might see in your local shops in Detroit or Denver. This is true for men's clothing too, in some cases. Don't be too surprised if you shop the entire mall and only find a couple of things that really work for your taste. Or, that what you do find is much more expensive (for the same product) than what you'd expect to pay back home.

A popular lingerie store in Albrook Mall

You may recall that very little is manufactured in Panama. Thus, anything shipped in to the country has a big shipping price tag attached to it, which accounts for part of that higher price. There used to be an import tax applied, as well, but in the case of goods manufactured in the U.S., some of those import tax fees on items priced less than $100 have been eliminated (as of 2013), thanks to a benefit provided as part of the recent U.S.-Panama Free Trade Agreement.

A recent example of the higher pricing is a Black & Decker blender, which retailed for $130 in Conway; online, the same model lists for $89.

Due to the price differences and the differences in our particular tastes, we found ourselves doing the bulk of our personal shopping for clothes and shoes on our trips back to the States.

Panama allows travelers to bring up to $2,000 in purchased goods back with them on return flights without charging local or import taxes on those goods. Realistically, Customs officials never seem to pay too much attention to this when you re-enter the country after traveling. So, as long as you remove price tags, who's to say that you didn't buy those things on some other trip? (Maybe it would be obvious if they checked that you took two bags when you left, and returned with three, but currently, there's little coordination or oversight of that type thing between Customs and the airlines.)

Taking Advantage of Someone Else's Treasures: The Secondhand Market

In a culture where expats come and go every few years, there are surprisingly few resources for making your hard-earned dollar go a little further on these types of purchases. But there are two, which are worth mentioning and may be good resources for you, as you look at relocating into this tropical environment.

Dejavu
Furniture with history
203-8095
www.dejavupanama.com
El Cangrejo neighborhood

This delightful little shop is a consignment store for furniture and lighting. The owner, Kristin Dove, is a good friend of mine. She's an expat from the U.S., who relocated to Panama years ago and married a local guy. She is passionate about repurposing furniture and providing great deals on the gently-used pieces she carefully chooses from expats (and locals) who are moving out of country or whose style has changed. And, if and when you leave Panama, be sure to contact Dejavu to help you get rid of the things you don't want to take with you.

Promises and Treasures S.A.
270-7457
Calle 74 East, San Francisco

This shop is owned by Roz, a delightful U.S. expat who came to teach in the Canal Zone three decades ago and then married a local businessman. She takes women's clothing, shoes and accessories and sells them out of this local retail store in San Francisco. Well-connected to Panama's well-heeled locals, the shop is lucky to receive a great selection of very nice name brands and styles. Admirably, proceeds from sales benefit a number of local non-profits and charities. This is a great place to find that perfect cocktail or long party dress that's only been worn once (and that you will likely only wear once, on Panama's formal circuit).

14

THE FIFTY SHADES OF PANAMA

Shopping for Guna Indian molas at the El Valle market

N O DOUBT MANY of you are familiar with the Fifty Shades of Grey trilogy published by E.L. James in 2011. But what I refer to here – as the fifty shades of Panama – has nothing to do with love and lust. It has to do with friendship.

When you move to Panama as an expat, it's obviously a whole lot different than moving to another city in your home country. Unless you're coming from another Spanish speaking country, the language is different from your own. The climate is, for most of us, very different, with high humidity that makes your clothes stick to you the minute you walk out the door. The lush scenery is spectacular, with fifty shades of green, especially during the month of November during the height of the rainy season.

But an aspect that makes Panama *really* special is the friendships you'll forge here. You may be familiar with the tagline that the Tourism Authority used until recently for marketing Panama – *Where the World Meets*, and the one that the Canal promotes (or did for a time) – *Gateway to the World*. The Panama America Chamber of Commerce markets itself as the *Business Gateway to the Americas*. From its geographic position alone, Panama is certainly a global meeting point.

What that means for you – in business and your personal life alike – is that you have a unique opportunity to get to know people from around the world.

When we lived in the U.S., most of our friends were from the U.S. In Panama, I was fortunate to meet and become friends with people from Belgium, Canada, Chile, Colombia, Ecuador, England, France, Ireland, Nicaragua, Scotland, Venezuela, and that's just to name a few.

The norm for my encounters with people in just one week in Panama often looked like this: a new colleague at work hailed from Bolivia; new neighbors in our building were from Chile; a lovely couple from Venezuela joined our social club; and a new business lead came from New Zealand. You get the picture.

Meeting people from around the globe opens up discussions and conversations that you might never have had before you moved to Panama.

By getting to know others you meet here, you experience the culture that formed them. Just by being with other world citizens, you may eat their food, sample their native drink, and hear tales of their lives before they came to Panama. And, they in turn get the same from you. Just by *being*, you're learning and absorbing other cultures. All of this enriches our lives.

Panama is truly a global meeting point. Not just for business, but for life. My grandmother used to tell me, "Variety is the spice of life." And she was right. Using that analogy, Panama is a very spicy place.

For the variety of friendships I formed and the other cultures I became familiar with in Panama, I am a wealthy person. In a few months time after moving to Panama, I'm sure you can say the same.

The fifty shades of Panama are truly the friendships you'll make, the people you'll meet, and the cultures you'll experience that you would never have had access to, in your home country.

In this way, Panama truly has something to offer everyone – you only need to open your eyes and step outside your door to find it.

ADDITIONAL PHOTO CREDITS:

Individual photos provided by others are noted in specific chapters, except for the following (because this contributor had several).

Tourist Mary Elie, who visited Panama in 2013, was kind enough to grant the use of her photos in these chapters:

Native children, Chapter 7

Embera Indian village, Chapter 12

A tipica meal, Chapter 13

Shopping for Guna Indian molas, Chapter 14

ABOUT THE AUTHOR

JuliAnne Murphy is a best-selling author, writer, speaker and businesswoman. She and her family relocated to the Republic of Panama in 2008 for business purposes. While the first two years of expat life was a tough transition for her, she grew to enjoy living in Panama and chose to stay even after her work contract ended.

JuliAnne began writing as a hobby in mid-2011, and her initial book was the first bestseller in the **The Gringo Guide to Panama** series: *The Gringo Guide to Panama: What to Know Before You Go.* Currently at work on her third book, Murphy lives in Costa Rica.

JuliAnne is a lover of life; she loves to travel, eat well, socialize, paddle board, read and do yoga. The things she misses most about Panama are early breakfasts at the Bayview Resort in El Palmar on a Saturday morning with her nose in her laptop, endless walks in Panama Pacifico with her dog Lily tracking Toucans and gato solos, house calls from her manicurist Pilar, and Sunday evening sunsets at the Balboa Yacht Club.

To learn more of her adventures in life,
visit www.PanamaGringoGuide.com,
www.LivinglaPuraVida.co, and
www.JuliAnneMurphy.com

Follow JuliAnne Murphy in social media:

 On Twitter:
https://twitter.com/JuliAnneMurph

 On YouTube:
www.Youtube.com/user/GringoGuidetoPanama

View the Photos in Full-Color!
To enjoy the photos in The Gringo Guide to Panama: More to Know Before You Go in full-color, get the Amazon Kindle version of this book.

Made in United States
Orlando, FL
01 April 2022

16403037R00147